THE ECO ATI

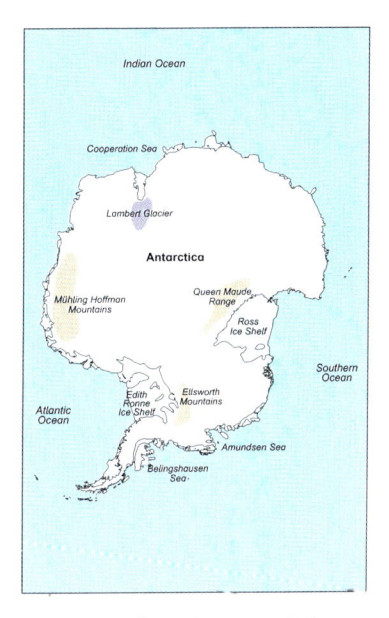

Written by Antony Mason

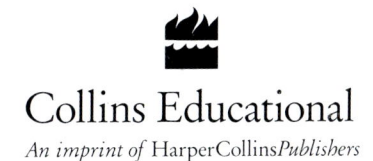

Collins Educational
An imprint of HarperCollinsPublishers

Contents

The Fragile Earth	3
Dilemmas and Solutions	5
The British Isles	10
Western Europe	12
Central Europe, the Balkans and Scandinavia	14
Russia	16
The Middle East and Central Asia	18
South Asia	20
China, Korea and Japan	22
South-east Asia and Papua New Guinea	24
North Africa, West Africa and the Sahel countries	26
Central Africa, East Africa and Southern Africa	28
Canada and Alaska	30
USA	32
Mexico, Central America and the Caribbean	34
Northern South America and Brazil	36
Southern South America	38
Australia	40
New Zealand and the Pacific Islands	42
Arctic (and Greenland) and Antarctica	44
Glossary	46
Index	47

THE FRAGILE EARTH

ONE WORLD

The ancient Chinese believed that everything in the world is connected: a fish in a pond is connected to the plants on the banks, and to winds over the ocean and the rocks in a mountain. It was like seeing the world as a vast and complex jigsaw puzzle: tiny pieces fit together to form a whole.

Scientific study points to the same conclusion. For example, the eruption of the Mount St Helens in the western USA in 1980, poured volcanic ash into the air which affected the weather of the whole planet for several years. This demonstrates that pollution in one country can affect the **environment** of its neighbours – if not the whole planet. River pollution, **acid rain**, the release of gases that harm the **ozone** layer – these don't respect national borders – they are international problems. The whole world is the environment – and environmental issues affect the whole world.

NATURAL FORCES

Life on earth is fragile, and human activities can destroy and pollute. Generally, however, natural forces are far more powerful and destructive to the world than anything humans can produce. The largest volcanic eruptions are many times more violent that the explosion of the largest nuclear bomb. Hurricanes can flatten forests at a single stroke and sweep away whole shorelines. Earthquakes have killed over two million people in the last 30 years. Floods, drought, disease, epidemics, grassland fires ignited by lightning – all can cause massive destruction and have an environmental impact.

HUMAN IMPACT

It can be argued that the world would be a better, more harmonious place without humans – or with fewer humans. In fact, the world did have fewer humans in the past, but it was no more harmonious. Nature is composed of hunters and the hunted, and countless animal and plant species became extinct long before humans trod the earth.

But humans do have an impact on the earth. Natural forces may be more powerful, but human activities can make natural disasters far worse. By destroying trees and plants in the dry regions around the deserts, for example, we allow the deserts to grow. By cutting down mountain forests, which hold back the rain and melting snows, we can cause worse flooding in the valleys below. There is also serious concern that industrial pollution may actually be affecting the world's climate, making it ever warmer.

Human population

There are now five billion people in the world, more than ever before. We are gradually taking up more space, using more and more of the earth's resources, and producing more waste. And the population of the world is still growing fast – there may be ten billion people by the year 2050.

There have been warnings in the past that the world will be unable to produce enough food to feed the growing population. So far, however, farmers have managed to keep producing sufficient quantities. But can they go on doing this for ever?

The control of population growth is a complex issue. In general, families tend to be larger in poorer countries, so children can earn money, and can help to look after their parents when they become old. Many countries are trying to encourage families to have fewer children, for instance, China, where families are asked to have just one child; but despite this, world population continues to grow.

Natural resources

Life in a modern, industrialized country uses a complicated web of goods and supplies – from breakfast cereals and refrigerators to motor cars, telephones, video games, medicines, and so on. These all depend on natural resources for the raw materials from which they are made, for example, grain and potatoes, timber, iron ore, crude oil and natural gas.

The increase in human population has resulted in greater use of natural resources and a need for more mines, oil wells, and fuel, and more roads and airports to transport the goods. We need more food: so scientists are now developing new, more productive strains of crops using **genetic engineering** and other techniques.

Can we go on demanding more and more of these things forever? The answer is probably, yes. Humans are usually able to find solutions when necessary, so, although one day the oil will run out, scientists will probably have discovered other fuels to use instead.

But what kind of world will it be? Will it be stripped of trees and wild animals, and covered with roads and airports, and greenhouses producing genetically-engineered, high-yield foods? What kind of world do we want to live in?

We need to find a balance – a balance between human needs and demands, and what the earth can provide with the least damage.

Pollution

Industrialized societies produce vast quantities of waste. Much is **biodegradable** and the processes of nature allow it to rot away and disintegrate harmlessly. Much, for example, glass, aluminium and paper, can be **recycled** and reused. But some of it – such as most plastics – is neither biodegradable nor recyclable and will remain for ever. And some of it – such as chemicals, old medicines, car oil – may cause harm and pollute the environment.

Industrial pollution has increased 100 times over this century. Some is extremely harmful to the environment and has to be discarded with great care. It cannot simply be poured away, and burning waste creates gases which are released into the air and can be equally dangerous.

It is also very difficult to control the pollution of millions of households which may be equally damaging. We all have a responsibility towards the environment.

A wind farm in Mid Glamorgan

DILEMMAS AND SOLUTIONS

SUSTAINABLE YIELDS

Every year, great shoals of fish in the sea produce eggs, which grow into young fish, which produce eggs, and so on. This makes fish a sustainable resource. If too many fish are caught, however, the shoals will become gradually smaller. Modern trawler fishing can catch huge quantities of fish with the result that many of the world's seas have been **overfished**. In some places fishing has had to stop altogether because there are simply not enough fish left to catch.

One solution is to catch only as many fish as can be replaced by the shoals, so the shoals remain large. This limited catch is called a **sustainable yield** – the fish can sustain the loss of all those caught, and will recover their numbers – so the shoals remain about the same size for ever.

The same principle can be applied to the timber trade. The trees cut down should be replaced by newly planted trees, and they should not be cut down faster than the time it takes for mature trees to replace them. There are about 10,000 km^2 of suitably managed forestry in the world – but there should be at least forty times this area if the world's timber consumption is to be properly supported.

Alternative energy

Electricity is produced at power stations, usually by burning **fossil fuels** such as oil and coal. Burning fossil fuels causes pollution and produces the dangerous **greenhouse gases** that may be making the earth warmer. But there are other sources of energy that are less damaging to the environment. Using natural power, for example, the wind, energy of waves or sea tides, or **solar energy**, causes very little pollution and is also cheap and renewable. As yet, however, the equipment is expensive and cannot produce enough energy for the world's needs. But these may be the clean, safe alternatives of the future.

Water

Plants and crops depend on water to grow and places starved of water for too long become deserts. Clean drinking water is essential for good health and to avoid disease, so access to supplies of clean water may become increasingly vital as the world's population grows, and this may be the most important environmental issue of the future.

Parks and reserves

There are still forests, mountains, remote islands and deserts that are not inhabited. Gradually, however, people are moving into these regions, to farm, to build on, to extract timber, oil or other minerals. This threatens to destroy the natural balance of the environment, by changing the landscape and removing trees and plants. And animals may well be threatened as their **habitat** changes.

Steps have been taken to save unspoilt places by protecting them as parks or **nature reserves**, where no development is permitted, and parks now cover 3% of the total land area of earth.

Being green

During the 1970s, it was discovered that the lead in petrol exhaust fumes (used to make engines run more smoothly) could cause various illnesses. But it was found that lead-free or unleaded petrol worked just as well in cars with specially converted engines and so many people changed to lead-free.

Other options to help keep the environment clean include using **green** biodegradable products rather than chemical products, such as bleach or detergents, and separating out recyclable waste.

Environmental organizations

There are a number of organizations which tackle some of the big environmental issues facing the world – such as industrial pollution, overfishing, rainforest destruction, and saving **endangered species**. Among these are Greenpeace, Friends of the Earth, and the World Wide Fund for Nature.

ENDANGERED SPECIES

Since life began on earth, thousands of species of animals and plants have become extinct. But today, plants and animals appear to be becoming extinct at an alarming speed. In the 20th century alone, 70 species of bird and 50 species of mammal have died out and at the current rate, half the world's species of plants and animals could become extinct in the next century – largely due to human activities. This would dramatically reduce the variety of living things in the world – the earth's **biodiversity**.

In the recent past various animals became extinct because of hunting. This is what happened to the dodo, the large flightless bird of Mauritius. And to the passenger pigeon, which was one of the commonest birds of the USA: in 1880 there were three billion but by 1914 there were none. Rare animals are still hunted for their skin, fur, shells or meat, or are captured for zoos or to be sold as pets. The trade in such animals and animal products has been outlawed in most parts of the world, and by agreements such as the Convention on International Trade in Endangered Species (**CITES**) – but it still goes on. Pollution and poisoning by **pesticides** and **toxic waste** is also responsible for animal deaths. But the biggest threat to many animals is loss of habitat or the destruction of their environment.

Most animals have a highly specialized way of living. Birds, for instance, eat a certain kind of food and make their nests in particular places. If these places are destroyed, and their food disappears, they cannot survive. Natural environments are complex webs of animals, plants and landscape. If one element in that web is damaged or destroyed, it can have a knock-on effect on everything living within it.

Animals threatened by extinction are called endangered species. In some cases there may be just a few animals of a species left, in others there may still be several thousand. In all cases, however, they are becoming rare enough to cause concern.

Endangered species can be saved. They can be protected from hunters and predators in the wild, and they can be protected in zoos or parks and encouraged to breed there – a process called **captive breeding**. When enough young animals have been born in captivity, some of them may be released back into the wild.

Many kinds of plants are endangered as well and need protecting equally.

GLOBAL WARMING

Records of the world's temperatures have been taken for over a hundred years, and scientists are beginning to get an idea of what the 'normal' temperatures of the world should be. Over the last century, the world's temperatures have been gradually getting warmer. If this continues there could be serious changes in the world climate. The polar ice caps could begin to melt, raising the level of the sea and flooding low-lying land and islands. This could also affect the ocean currents, which have an important influence on the climates of many parts of the world.

This '**global warming**' may be part of a natural cycle caused by earth's orbit, but many scientists believe that human activity is responsible. Burning fossil fuels and rainforests, and producing industrial pollution, fills the atmosphere with carbon dioxide. Normally the sun's heat escapes out of the atmosphere, but carbon dioxide traps it in. The result is that the world is becoming surrounded by a kind of greenhouse of gas which keeps it warmer – the '**greenhouse effect**'.

It is still not clear whether global warming is caused by human activity – but if it is we need to act quickly to control the **greenhouse gases** before it is too late, and before the climate changes beyond repair.

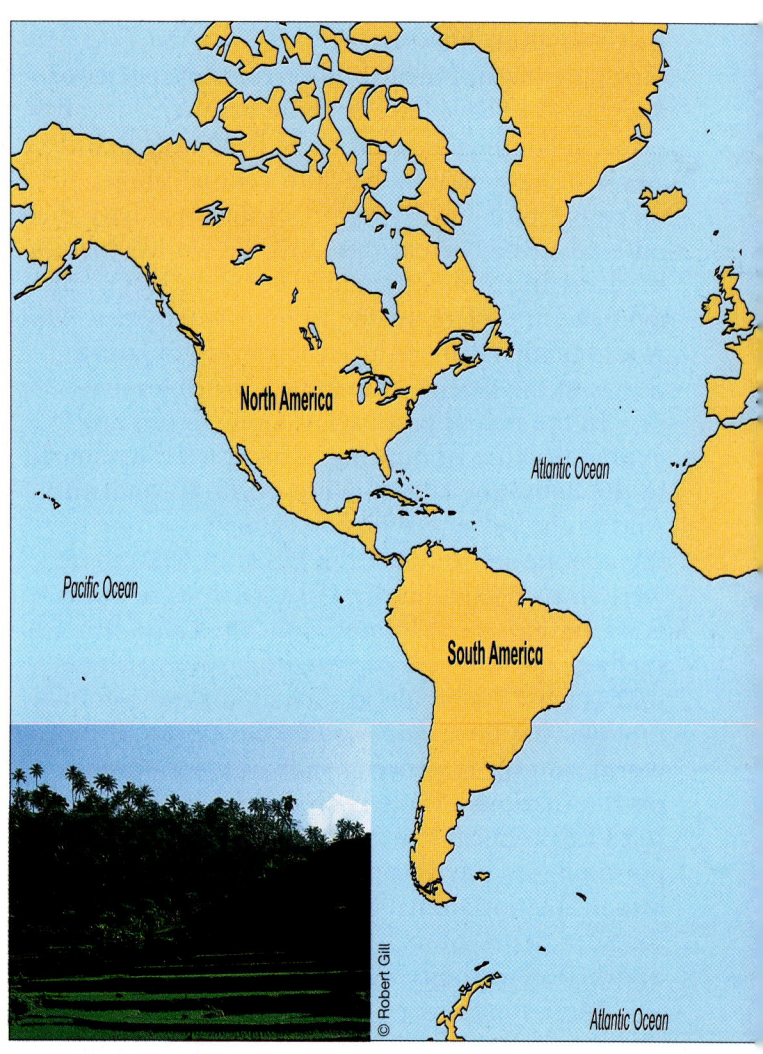

Paddy Fields in Bali

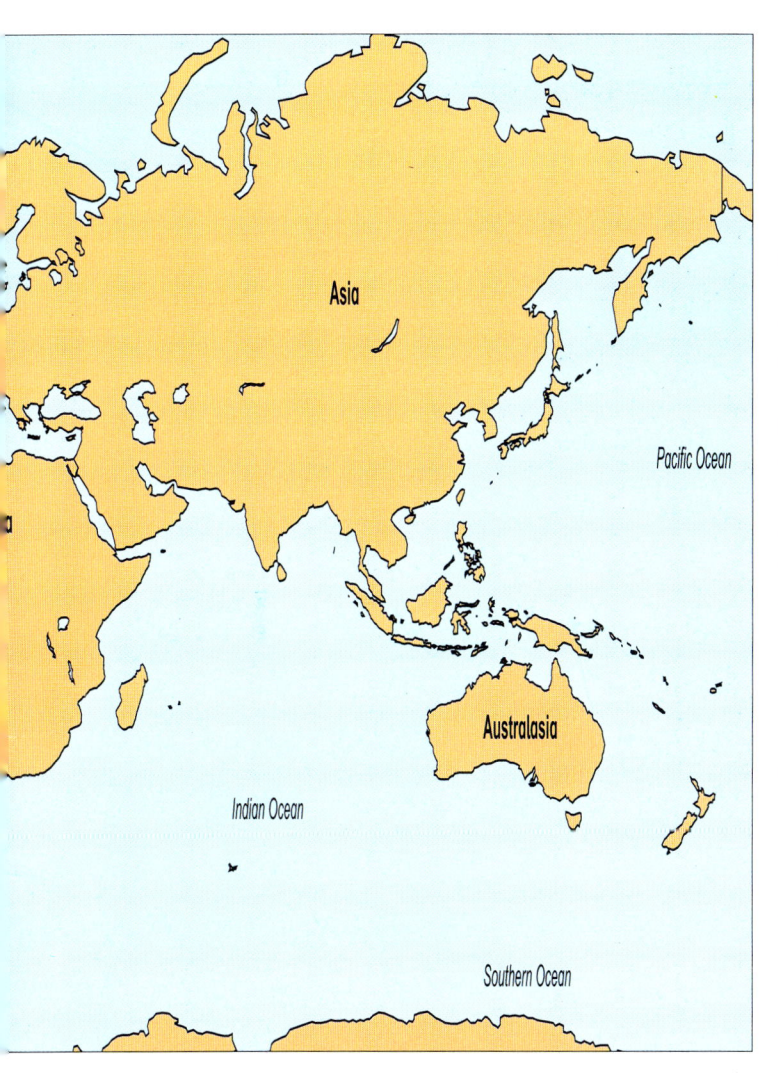

SAVING THE WHALES

Whales are the largest mammals on earth, but mainly feed on small sea creatures. From earliest times they have been hunted, but during the 19th and early 20th century, hunting increased rapidly. Whaling boats became bigger, their harpoons more powerful. There was also an increasing demand for whale products – especially the oil from their blubber, which was made into margarine, and the plastic-like baleen (whalebone). In 1930 alone, 30,000 blue whales were killed. By the 1970s, it looked as though the blue whale, humpback, fin and sperm whale were on the verge of extinction. A massive campaign was waged by **environmentalists** against whaling. The whale-hunting nations themselves had to admit that there was a crisis – they were now catching fewer and fewer whales. In 1982 the International Whaling Commission agreed to stop most whaling for a time to allow whales to recover their numbers. The whales were saved – although several kinds have only small populations and remain endangered. Japan and Norway still kill a number of whales for 'scientific purposes' – but would like to kill more. Saving the whale was a great environmental victory but – as with so many environmental issues – the battle is not yet over.

The British Isles

Traffic on the M25

St John's Lock, the River Thames

Animal at risk

There are over 100 endangered species in the British Isles. One of them is the minute snail called Desmoulin's whorl, which is no bigger than a grain of rice. It became famous in 1996 when some were found in Berkshire, in a field where a new bypass road was to be built around the town of Newbury. Although the road project was costing many millions of pounds, its progress had to be reconsidered, or at least altered, so that this population of a rare, tiny snail could be protected.

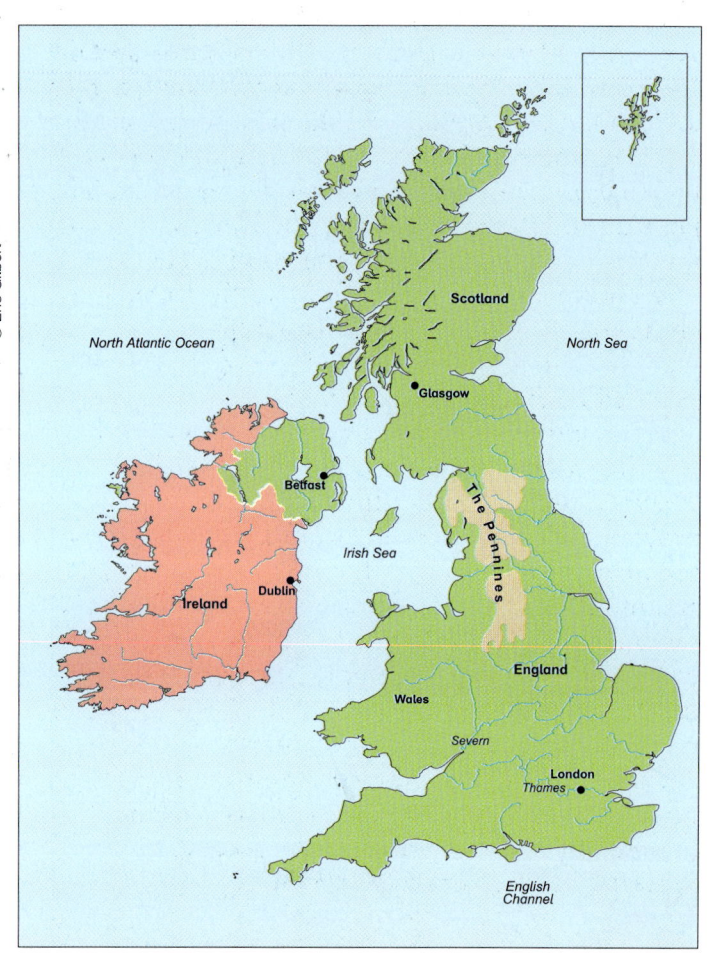

Great Britain was the first country in the world to develop factories to mass-produce manufactured goods. The Industrial Revolution began during the 18th century, and by the 1800s industry was beginning to change the look of the countryside and the way people lived.

The Industrial Revolution brought many of the environmental problems that we see today. The population increased, and the poor, many without their own land to farm, left the countryside to work in towns and cities. They usually rented cheap rooms in small back-to-back houses, without drainage or water, and breathed air polluted by factory chimneys.

During the 20th century, living conditions have improved, and people became generally wealthier and healthier. But there are new problems. Great Britain has a large population and the roads are crowded with traffic. Power stations and industries create pollution as they produce more energy and more goods. To maintain levels of food production, farmers use chemicals on the fields to produce ever more crops. The health scare surrounding BSE (bovine spongiform encephalopathy) arose directly from an effort to produce more beef and beef products, such as gelatine, by unnatural means – by feeding vegetarian cattle with meat products.

Traffic

Air pollution in the cities, caused largely by the exhaust gases from vehicles, can result in asthma and other health problems. More and more cars are produced and sold every year. At the present rate, the crowded parts of England will have a third more cars within the next 15 years, increasing pollution and traffic jams. The way to prevent this is to develop public transport, and to encourage people to leave their cars at home. But few people want to give up their own car.

The River Thames

Great Britain has plenty of rivers, which supply us with drinking water, fish, a means of travel and beautiful places to enjoy. But life in the rivers can be wiped out by poisonous waste that is illegally poured into rivers from factories, or by chemicals that are washed into rivers from farmland. However, polluted rivers can recover. Thirty-five years ago the River Thames in London was so polluted that there were no fish in it. After many years of careful work, the river has become much cleaner, and over 50 species of fish have returned to it.

WESTERN EUROPE

Pine trees killed by acid rain

Animal at risk

The Spanish imperial eagle is a magnificent bird of prey. Over the centuries, hunters, farmers and egg-collectors have reduced its numbers, and now only a few dozen pairs survive in the wild. They are found only in protected areas, such as the Coto Doñana nature reserve on the south-western coast of Spain. Strict laws have been introduced to protect them, and some have also been bred in captivity, so they may have escaped the threat of extinction.

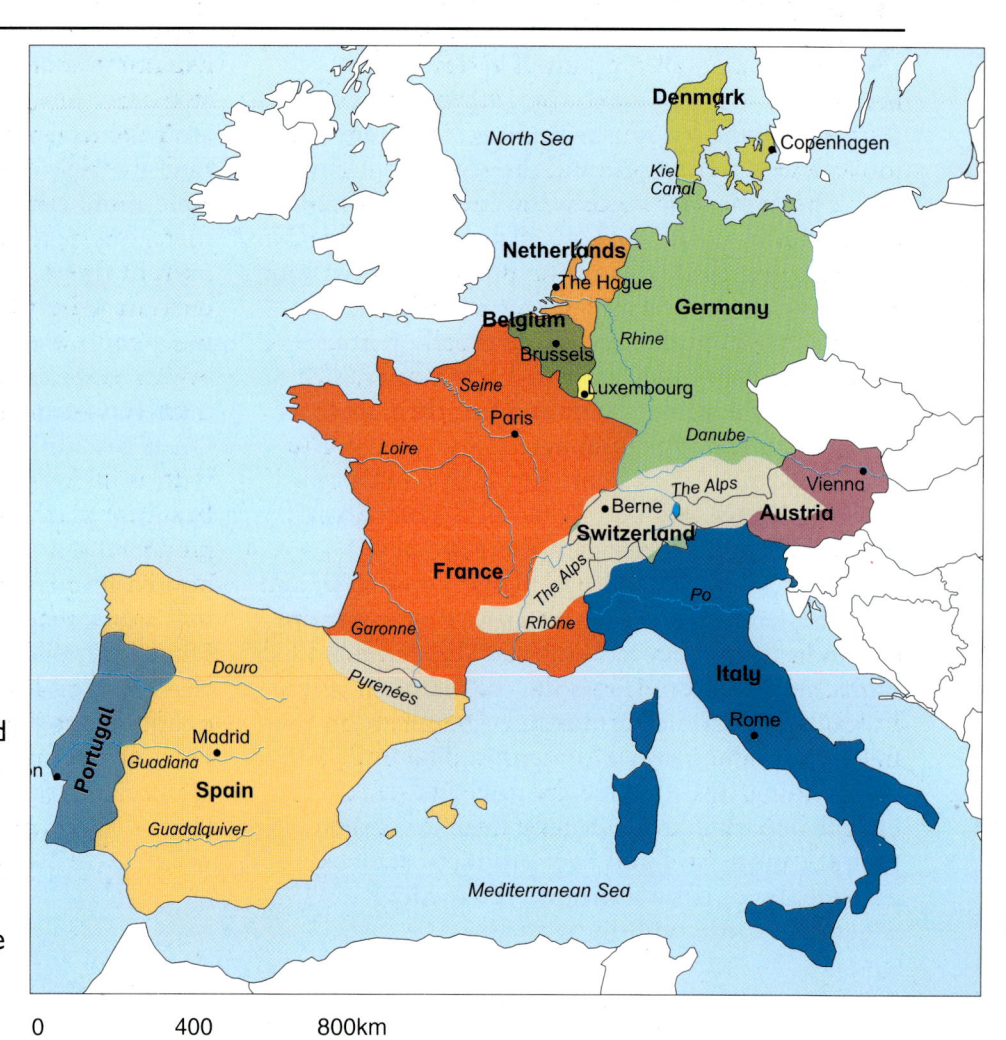

Western Europe is a wealthy part of the world. It has rich farming land, and plenty of prosperous industries, manufacturing goods from jam to aircraft. Its farmers produce easily enough food for everyone to eat – in fact it produces so much food that a lot of it is wasted. Compared to people in many other parts of the world, Western Europeans live well.

However, like all industrial parts of the world, Western Europe faces a number of serious environmental problems. The factories pollute the air and the rivers and the roads are crowded with traffic. The large and wealthy population demands more and better things and more space to live in, so large areas of the countryside have disappeared each year as more houses, shopping centres, roads and business parks are built.

In the past, European countries had to solve their own ecological problems. Now many of its countries are members of the European Union, which takes the **ecology** of Europe seriously. The EU brings all its member countries together to find solutions that benefit all of Europe and an international approach to the environment is essential – especially over problems such as air pollution and acid rain.

ACID RAIN

Factories, powers stations, cars and domestic heating systems all produce waste gases, which go into the atmosphere. When these gases combine with the moisture in the sky, sulphuric or nitric acid is formed. In the atmosphere, very mild acids are created but when the acid falls as rain, they are strong enough to damage trees and kill fish. Large areas of forest in Europe have been badly damaged by **acid rain**. One solution is to clean all waste gases with filters, but this is not always easy to organize, as the acid rain falling in one country may have been created by the factories of another.

CHEMICALS IN FARMING

In recent years, scientists have helped farmers produce more food by developing **fertilizers** to make the soil richer, and chemical pesticides to kill insects that eat the crops. But there is a price to pay for this kind of farming. The chemicals are expensive, and the produce may be less healthy and less tasty. The chemicals may kill useful insects as well as harmful ones, and may pollute rivers when rainwater flows off the fields and into streams. So many farmers are farming **organically** without chemicals and pesticides.

CENTRAL EUROPE, THE BALKANS AND SCANDINAVIA

A modern turf-roofed house in Lofoten, Norway

Animal at risk

The pollution of the world's seas is a growing problem – particularly the seas which are almost enclosed by land, such as the Black Sea and the Mediterranean Sea. Many sea animals and plants cannot survive if the water becomes dirty. Mediterranean monk seals have become extremely rare for several reasons: through hunting; being caught accidentally in fishing nets; being deprived of food through overfishing, and being poisoned by water pollution. They are shy animals and don't like to be disturbed. In the Mediterranean, they now live mainly on remote shores and specially protected reserves, while other groups live on the west coast of Africa.

This segment of Europe stretches from the Arctic north to the sunny Mediterranean countries of the south. The largest Scandinavian countries – Norway, Sweden and Finland – enjoy a high standard of living. Winters are cold and long, but there is plenty of farmland and open space. The central European countries, to the south of the Baltic Sea, share a very different history. From the end of the Second World War until the 1990s, Bulgaria, Romania, Hungary, the Czech Republic, Poland, and countries to the east of them, were ruled by the Soviet Union – a group of Communist countries dominated by Russia. The Soviet Union aimed to produce plenty of cheap goods from huge farms and factories. But the factories were old-fashioned, producing poor-quality goods and huge quantities of pollution. Since the early 1990s, these East European countries have been independent, but it will take time before newer, better and cleaner industries are created.

The countries on the tongue of land between the Adriatic Sea and the Black Sea are known as the Balkans. Bosnia, Slovenia and Croatia once formed part of Yugoslavia. Since the early 1990s they have become independent, but the break-up of Yugoslavia resulted in war which, in turn, has had a destructive environmental impact, and will take many years to reverse.

CHERNOBYL

In 1986, a major accident occurred at the **nuclear power** station at Chernobyl in the Ukraine. The nuclear reactor exploded, and tonnes of radioactive waste poured into the air. About 5,000 people died as a direct result of the accident, and 30,000 people were injured by the **radioactive fallout**. **Radioactivity** causes diseases such as cancer, and remains in the soil for years. Huge areas of farmland around the power station were poisoned, and are still too dangerous to use. Many villages had to be abandoned and even farms in Wales, 2,000km away, were affected. The Chernobyl explosion has raised questions about whether nuclear power is too dangerous use.

LOW-ENERGY HOMES

The energy used to heat homes usually comes from burning oil, gas or coal, or from a power station, which makes electricity by also burning oil, gas or coal. Both deplete valuable resources and cause pollution. Energy use can be reduced by insulating the roof and sealing doors and windows to prevent loss of heat. In Scandinavia, experimental houses have been built which use no power at all for heat. They are so well-sealed that body heat is enough to keep them warm, even in winter.

Russia

Animal at risk

Wolves were once common throughout the northern hemisphere, including Europe. For centuries they were considered an enemy to humans, because they are skilled hunters. They commonly formed packs of up to 30 animals to kill deer and other wild animals, as well as sheep, cattle, horses and sometimes people. The grey wolves of Siberia have been killed as dangerous pests by farmers and foresters, and have also been trapped for their fur. They need large areas to hunt in, and so are affected by loss of habitat. Once found in huge numbers, there are only about 130,000 left, and most of these are in Russia.

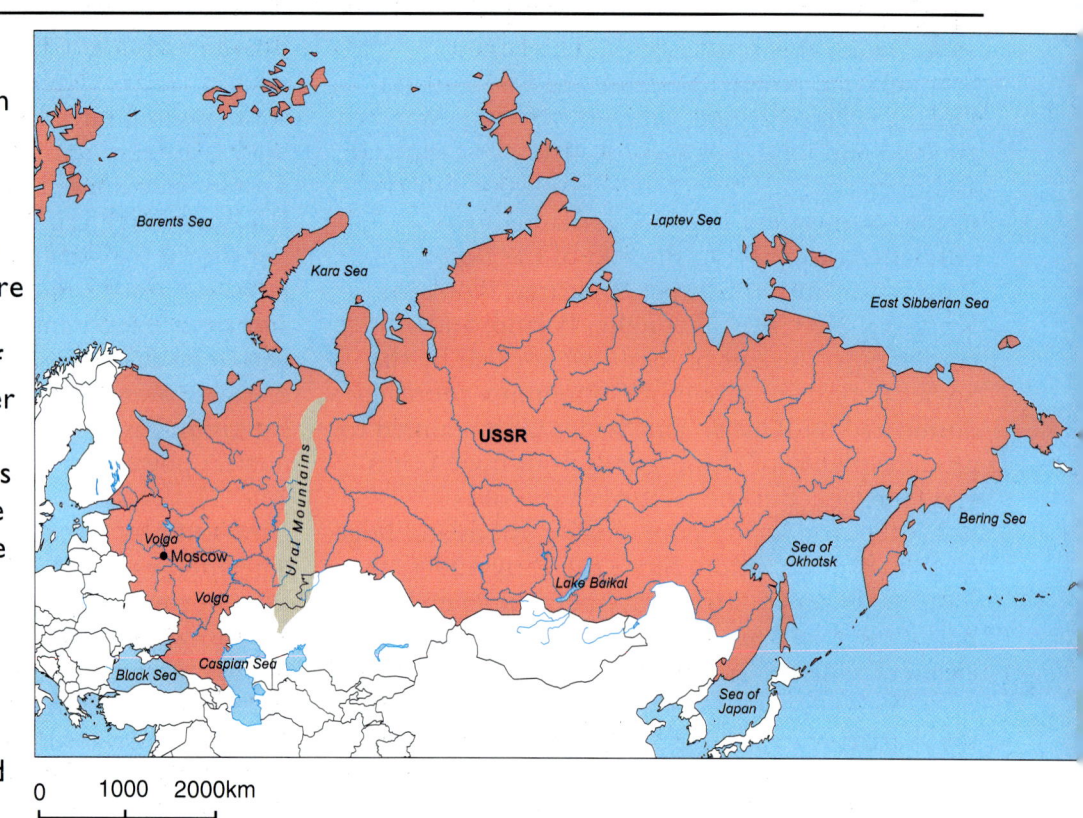

Russia is the largest country in the world. The western section of it (up to the Ural Mountains) is considered to be in Europe. The rest is in Asia. The Asian section consists mainly of Siberia, a vast expanse of forests and icy wastes that stretches thousands of kilometres to the Pacific Ocean. Until about 1990, Russia formed the main part of the Soviet Union. This included many countries of Eastern Europe (such as Ukraine) and Central Asia (such as Kazakhstan), which have now become independent.

Russia has some of the worst pollution in the world. In the huge industrial towns such as Perm, Novosibirsk and Magnitogorsk, old-fashioned factories pour out thick clouds of gases and many of the major rivers are severely polluted with industrial waste. Illnesses caused by pollution are common, and some babies are born with handicaps and deformed limbs.

Russian people are aware of the damage that pollution causes, but are able to do little to prevent it. As yet they cannot afford to buy better, more efficient cars, and the country cannot afford to build new and cleaner factories. Cleaning up the environment costs money, and Russia is not wealthy enough to do this.

INDUSTRIAL POLLUTION

All industries produce waste products. These might be paper and card and bits of metal. But they might include dangerous gases resulting from burning fuel to heat materials, such as iron ore to make steel, and poisonous chemical residue from chemical processes, for example, in making paint. All waste products must be treated very carefully or discarded in safe places to protect the environment. Dangerous gases and chemicals can cause serious illness, such as asthma and bronchitis. Near the industrial city of Astrakhan, the air is sometimes so bad that children have to wear gas masks.

LAKE BAIKAL

Lake Baikal is the world's deepest lake, with a depth of nearly 2km. It is the habitat of the world's only freshwater seal, the Baikal nerpa, as well as various, unique, species of fish and shrimps. The lake water was so pure that local people drank straight from it. In the 1960s, however, a factory opened at Baikalsk to produce cellulose from wood pulp to make paper and textiles, and much of the southern shoreline of the lake was damaged by **effluent** from the factory. Faced with outrage, the factory made great efforts to clean up, but some pollution still reaches the lake.

THE MIDDLE EAST AND CENTRAL ASIA

Desert farming – harvesting sugarcane

Animal at risk

The oryx is a large antelope from the desert regions of Arabia and northern Africa. It survives in the desert by extracting virtually all the water it needs from its food. Unfortunately, oryxes are easy to hunt with rifles and, in 1972, the last wild Arabian oryx was killed. But the Arabian oryx was not extinct: in 1962, three had been captured in the desert of Oman and taken to Phoenix Zoo in Arizona, and more were brought there from other zoos. In 1982, a herd of young oryxes bred in captivity was taken back to Oman, where they now live in a reserve – rescued from the brink of extinction.

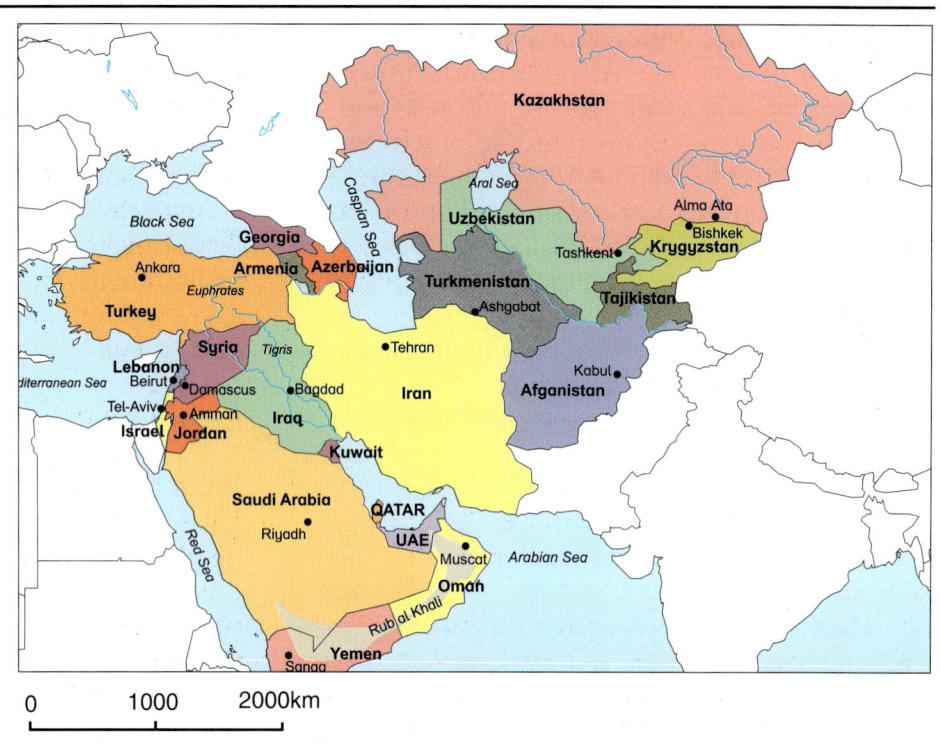

Much of this region is desert, from the towering sand dunes of the Rub' al Khali, or Empty Quarter, of southern Saudi Arabia, to the high, dry mountains of Afghanistan. Rain is rare and farmers use carefully-devised irrigation systems to take water to the fields in channels and pipes. Villages and towns grew up around oases, and along the fertile river valleys. Some of the world's first civilizations grew up in the valleys of the Rivers Tigris and Euphrates over 5,000 years ago.

There is enough rainfall for farming on the Mediterranean coast, in the mountains of Yemen, in Turkey and the Caucasus (the land between the Black Sea and the Caspian Sea) and much of Kazakhstan is covered by steppes, or rich grasslands. There are industries in the towns and cities. By far the most valuable product, however, is oil, and the natural gas that is found with it. In many countries of the Middle East and Central Asia, oil and natural gas are tapped and exported to other countries. These fuels are a vital source of energy, but also a great source of pollution. One of the world's greatest environmental disasters occurred during the Gulf War of 1990-91, when Iraqi soldiers set fire to the oil wells in Kuwait and poured thousands of tonnes of crude oil into the sea.

THE ARAL SEA DISASTER

Forty years ago, the Aral Sea was the fourth-largest inland sea in the world. Since the 1960s, huge irrigation schemes have been set up in the region, taking water from the rivers feeding the Aral Sea to fields of cotton in Uzbekistan, Kazakhstan and Turkmenistan. As a result the Aral Sea has shrunk to about half its former size. Most of the fish have died, and towns that were once ports on the shore are now many kilometres from the water. Wind now carries salt from the dried seabed and scatters it over the countryside, poisoning the land.

FARMING THE DESERT

Irrigation, using ditches and channels, for farming the desert usually carries water from a well or spring at an oasis. There is plenty of water under the desert, but most of it is too expensive to drill and pump out. Some of it is renewable: it comes from rain falling on distant mountains and travelling under the desert in layers of soft rock. Some is **fossil water**, trapped for thousands of years.

In a desert irrigation scheme, four litres of water may evaporate in the heat to every litre used by the plants. The precious water can be preserved by growing crops in plastic polytunnels to trap moisture, and by dripping water onto the soil, reducing evaporation.

SOUTH ASIA

Animal at risk

A hundred years ago there were 40,000 tigers in India; by 1972, there were fewer than 2,000. Most of these had been killed by hunters, and by villagers who were frightened of this large and powerful cat. Tigers also suffered from loss of habitat, which reduced the number of animals they could hunt and eat, such as antelope and wild pigs. In 1973, India began 'Project Tiger': a series of 18 special reserves was set up where wild tigers were protected. In the safety of these reserves, the number of wild tigers has now risen to over 4,000.

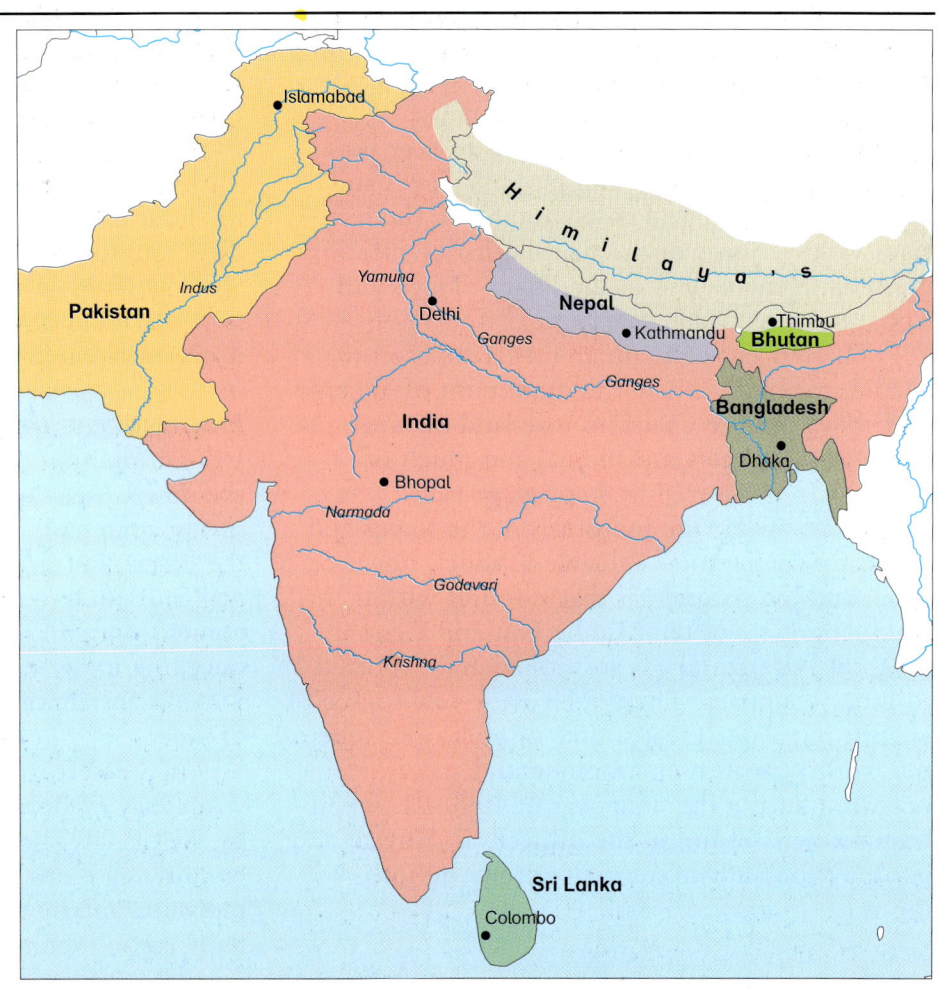

20

This region of Asia is framed by the Himalayan and Karakoram mountains in the north, and by the warm waters of the Indian Ocean in the south. These are some of the most heavily populated and varied countries in the world. India contains tropical rainforest, desert, mountains, quiet rural villages and huge, industrial cities. With 900 million people, its population is second in size only to China.

Most people live by farming, and India and Pakistan now produce enough food to feed their own people. Most areas have enough water, and each year the wet season brings heavy rains with the monsoon winds.

Over the past century many of the forests have been cut down for use in industry. The loss of forests in the north has had a disastrous effect on Bangladesh. Without the forests to hold back the water, rain in the mountains sweeps down to the rivers and causes flooding in the lowlands where the Rivers Ganges and Jamuna (or Brahmaputra) join to form a delta. Devastating cyclones also cause flooding. Over 450,000 people have been killed in floods in Bangladesh during the last 30 years.

Poverty increases environmental problems – firewood is burned for fuel, and old cars and factories cause high levels of pollution. And sadly, these problems are expensive to solve.

THE TRAGEDY OF BHOPAL

In December 1984, there was a terrible accident at the American-owned factory, Union Carbide, in the city of Bhopal in central India. A large quantity of poisonous gas (methyl isocyanate) leaked out, killing 2,500 people and injuring about 50,000 others. During an investigation, it was found that the factory had very low safety standards. High safety standards, however, are more expensive and it seems that greater risks are taken with safety in poorer countries, in order to produce cheaper goods.

THE GREEN REVOLUTION

Forty years ago, many Asian countries were in constant danger of **famine**. During the 1960s, new farming methods were applied using strains of **hybrid seeds**, producing more food and resisting disease and pests. The land was enriched by using chemical fertilizers, and pests were killed using pesticides. The Punjab, in India, could produce twice the amount of wheat after just 20 years. However, this **green revolution** of new farming methods had disadvantages. The materials were expensive and some chemicals made farmworkers ill, and damaged useful insects.

CHINA, KOREA AND JAPAN

A birth control poster in China

Animal at risk

Giant pandas may look like bears but, in fact, they are probably relatives of racoons. They live deep in the bamboo forests of Yunnan and Sichuan provinces where they eat mainly bamboo shoots – as much as 23kg a day. For many years, pandas have been hunted for their fur, and the special forests where they find their food have become smaller and smaller as more land is taken over for farming. Sometimes large areas of bamboo flower and then die, leaving pandas with nothing to eat. As a result there are only about 1,200 pandas left in the wild. They now live mainly in protected reserves.

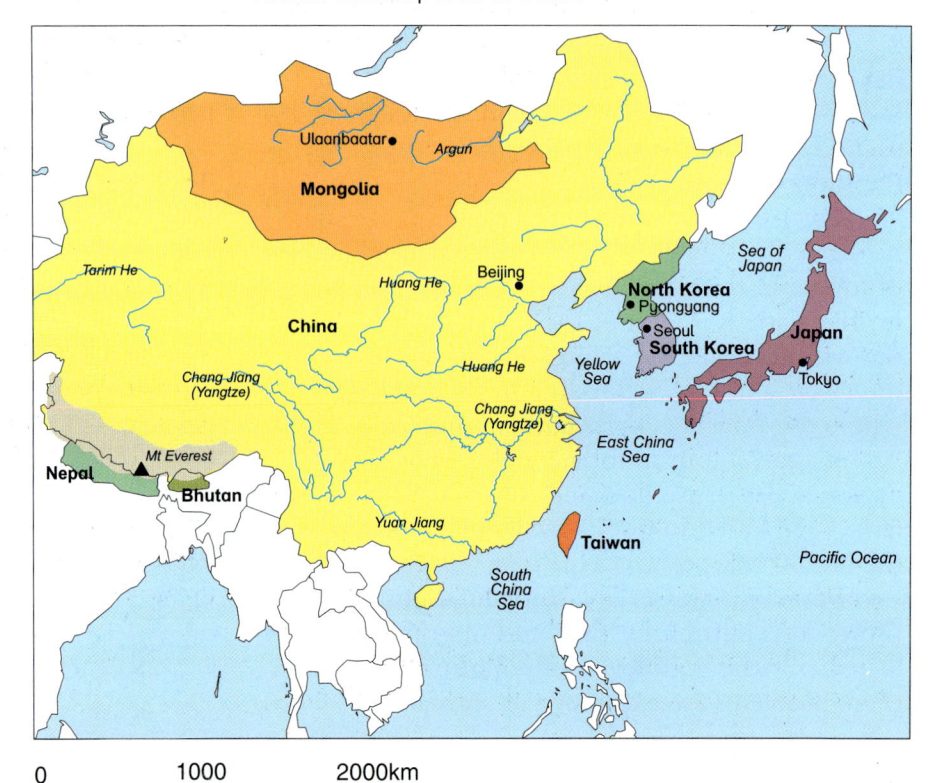

China has the largest population in the world: 1,205 million people. Almost all these people live in the east of China, and most of the rest of this large country is covered by remote mountains and desert. Many of the big cities are industrial centres, surrounded by factories making a vast range of goods that are sold all over the world, from toys to heavy machinery.

The biggest river in China is the Chang Jiang (or Yangtze Kiang). Over thousands of years this river has caused disastrous floods. Now the Chinese are building the largest hydroelectric dam in the world to control the river water and to produce electricity. The lake behind the dam will flood many villages, as well as some of the spectacular Yangtze Gorges. Some people argue that this will change the whole ecology of the Yangtze Valley, while the Chinese point to the advantages of controlling the floods and having a 'clean' source of energy.

Korea has been divided in two separate countries since the end of the Second World War in 1945. North Korea is a mysterious Communist country which is seldom visited by outsiders. By contrast, South Korea is a modern, fast-growing industrial nation. Its industries produce clothes, electronic goods, cars and ships, much for export.

To the east of both China and Korea lies one of the world's most successful industrial nations. Set in a group of four large islands and 3,000 smaller ones, Japan has grown rapidly since the Second World War, with leading industries producing hi-fi equipment, cameras, televisions and cars. Most of Japan's 125 million people live in the cities on the coasts, but many people still farm in the mountainous countryside. Fishing is also an important industry.

One child only

China's population is already over a billion. During the 1960s the government realized that China would face starvation if population growth did not slow down. The Chinese were encouraged to marry at an older age, and to have one only child. Even so, 50,000 babies are born every day in China and the population is still growing.

The Green Great Wall

One of the world's most remarkable monuments is the Great Wall of China, built to keep out warring tribes. Now another remarkable 'wall' is being built, made from living trees. Thousands of trees are being planted to keep out the Gobi Desert and the cold winds from Siberia in a Green Great Wall.

SOUTH-EAST ASIA AND PAPUA NEW GUINEA

Fishing craft, Vietnam

Jungle, Indonesia

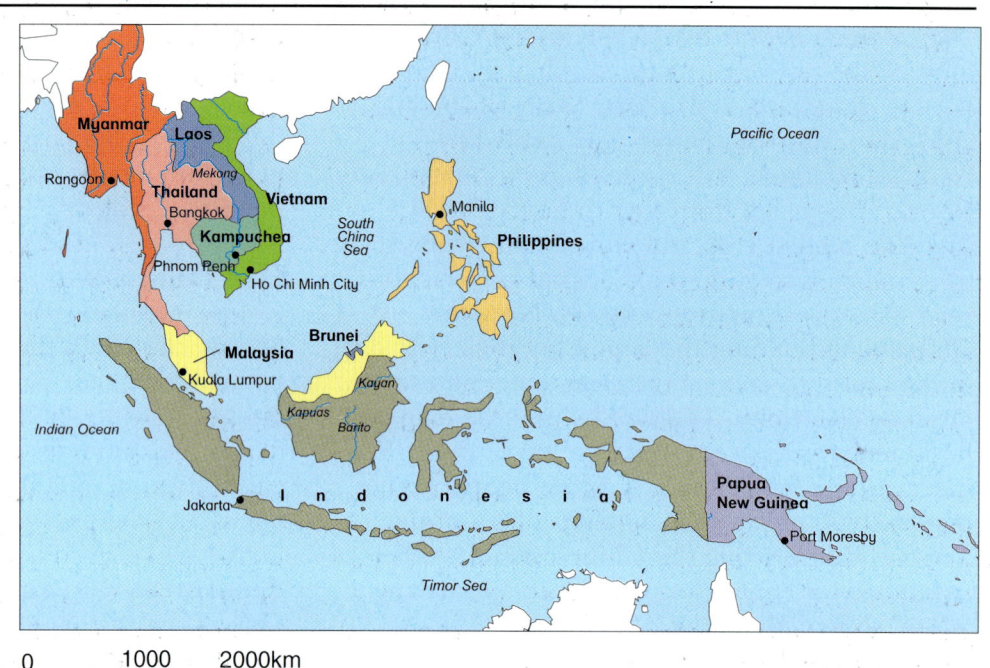

Animal at risk

All five kinds of rhinoceros in the world are threatened by extinction – and particularly the three Asian species: the Great Indian rhino, the Javan rhino, and the smaller Sumatran rhino. Only about 60 Javan rhinos are left in the wild, and most of these are in the Ujung Kulon reserve on the western tip of Java, although a small group was recently discovered living in Vietnam. Javan rhinos live on beaches and in the wooded marshlands, where they feed off the shoots of young trees. Like the Indian rhino, the Javan rhino has only one horn. Some people in the Far East believe that rhino horn makes effective medicine, and so many rhinos have been killed for their horn.

24

This lush region consists of a cluster of countries on the mainland of Asia, plus thousands of islands that lie scattered across the warm, tropical seas.

South-East Asia has developed in recent times into one of the fastest-growing regions of the world. The area is rich in raw materials, such as oil, coal, timber and tin and many of these are exported. Meanwhile Thailand, Malaysia, Indonesia and the Philippines have built up modern industries, manufacturing hi-tech electronic equipment, cars and toys. But the most developed and modern nation of the region is the tiny city state of Singapore – one of the world's most prosperous countries.

All the major industries of South-East Asia present dangers to the environment. Mining produces great gashes in the landscape and toxic waste; forestry removes irreplaceable trees and allows the soil to wash away; factories produce waste chemicals and gases that can poison the land and rivers.

Many people, living in rural villages, still farm and rice crops increased enormously during the green revolution. Even so, every year thousands of people leave the villages to go to the crowded cities, hoping to find work. The population of Jakarta, the capital of Indonesia, is growing at the rate of one million every three years – and it cannot really cope.

Pillaging the sea

The people of South-East Asia eat a great deal of seafood. However, in recent years there have been fewer and fewer fish to catch as a direct result of overfishing.

Close to land, coral reefs are being destroyed by industrial pollution and by rich farm fertilizer flowing into the sea from rivers. In some places dynamite is used to kill fish and to collect coral and shells to sell to tourists. Some people also use cyanide poison to stun tropical fish, to sell to people with aquariums.

Hardwoods

The rainforests of South-East Asia contain valuable hardwood timbers, such as mahogany, teak and ebony. Industries in Europe, the USA and Japan pay high prices for these woods. But the forests of South-East Asia have been disappearing at an alarming rate. In less than a century, South-East Asia has lost three quarters of its forests. In Malaysia some of the world's richest rainforests are being destroyed at a rate of 6,500km^2 every year.

One solution is to restrict logging to sustainable yields. Both Thailand and Indonesia have introduced various logging restrictions to save their forests.

NORTH AFRICA, WEST AFRICA AND THE SAHEL COUNTRIES

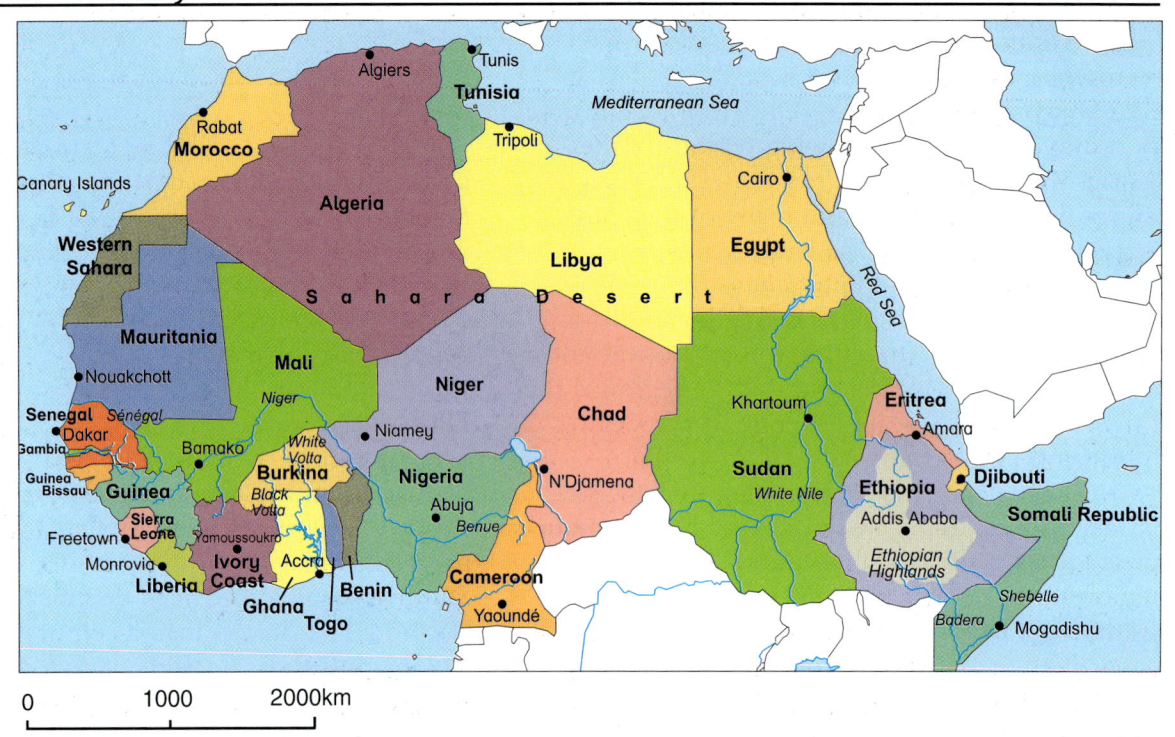

Animal at risk

There are huge herds of zebra in East Africa and southern Africa, so it may seem surprising to find zebras listed as an endangered species. However, there are three species of zebra: the plains zebra, the mountain zebra and Grevy's zebra. Grevy's zebra lives in the semi-desert of the Horn of Africa and is, in fact, the largest of them all, measuring 1.5m at the shoulder. It has been hunted for its skin and for food, and killed by the repeated droughts, and so it is now very rare. It is protected in some reserves in Kenya and Ethiopia.

The Sahara Desert, the largest desert in the world, covers most of northern Africa. The desert separates North Africa and the Mediterranean coast from the rest of Africa. As a result, North Africa is rather different to the rest of Africa. Once part of the Roman Empire, it was conquered by the Arabs, who brought Islam to the region. Most people live on the Mediterranean coast, in the green mountain valleys, or in the oases, where dates are the main crop.

A thousand years ago, Arab traders began to cross the desert to West Africa, and found lands rich in gold and ivory. Along the coasts and further south, towards the Equator, there is plenty of rain, and the land is green with forests and farm crops. But between this green land and the Sahara is a band of semi-desert called the Sahel, which stretches across Africa from Senegal to Sudan. Tough grasses, bushes and some trees can grow in the Sahel, and there is usually just enough rain to grow crops. Over the last 15 years, however, less rain has fallen on the Sahel, and as people and their goats destroy the trees, the desert moves closer. All the countries along the Sahel are now threatened by the growth of the desert.

The big cities of West Africa are mainly ports on the coast. Nigeria has large reserves of oil, but oil drilling has caused great environmental damage, particularly in Ogoniland. West Africa is also used as a cheap dumping ground for toxic waste from industrial countries in Europe and North America.

FAMINE IN THE HORN OF AFRICA

Over the last thirty years there have been a series of **famines** in Ethiopia and Somalia. These have occurred in the semi-desert regions, when droughts lasting several years left the people without food. In 1981–84, one million people died in Eritrea and Ethiopia and eight million came close to starvation. Cutting down trees for firewood has caused soil erosion; a growing population meant more mouths to feed; tribal warring caused destruction; and their larger herds of cattle and sheep ate the grass too quickly. In 1992–95, United Nations troops were sent to Somalia to stop the fighting so that aid could reach the starving people.

SOLAR ENERGY

Bringing water to crops in the Sahel requires energy to pump the water up from the ground and into the fields. Rather than use petrol or electricity, environmentally friendly solar power can be collected by solar panels and converted into electricity to run pumps and other equipment.

CENTRAL AFRICA, EAST AFRICA AND SOUTHERN AFRICA

Armed Ethiopians

Elephants in Kenya

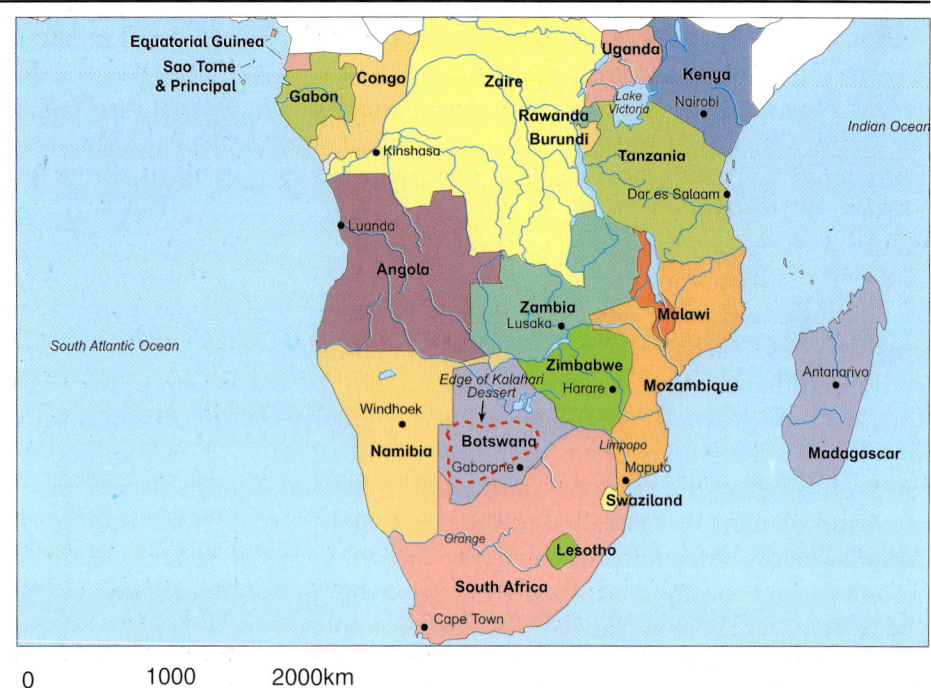

Animal at risk
There are only about 600 mountain gorillas in the world. About 300 are found in the volcanic Virunga mountains that line the borders between Zaire and Rwanda; and 300 are in Uganda to the north. They live peacefully in small family groups, feeding off plants and fruit and sleeping in large nests on the ground or in the trees. However, bit by bit the mountain forests have been cleared away for farming, and gorillas have been killed by hunters and caught to sell to zoos. This region has also been affected by the civil war in Rwanda: refugees fled to the mountains, and cut down thousands of trees for firewood.

The southern half of Africa contains a variety of landscapes, including the grasslands of East Africa, high mountains and volcanoes, tropical rainforests, swamplands and desert. There is also a huge range of wildlife, such as the giraffes, lions and zebras of the grasslands, the hippos, crocodiles and pelicans of the **wetlands**, and the unique wildlife of Madagascar, which includes the lemurs and numerous kinds of chameleon.

Each year thousands of tourists visit Africa to admire the wildlife. But to many people who live here, wildlife is often a problem. Most people live by farming and fishing and they need the land for cattle and crops. Each year, wildlife is pushed back into smaller areas, and the number of animals is reduced by hunting and loss of habitat.

The region's industries are found mainly in the big cities. Apart from South Africa, however, these countries do not have much heavy industry. A greater threat to the environment comes from forestry and mining. Many of these countries have forests of valuable timber, and diamonds, copper and other metals which are exported to bring much-needed income. But forestry and mining can be extremely damaging to the environment. Up to 5,000km^2 of forest is lost each year in Zaire alone.

WAR AND CIVIL WAR

Most of the countries of Africa have become independent since the Second World War. For many, such as Uganda, Angola and Mozambique, independence has followed wars and civil wars. Many people have been killed, and many made homeless. Roads and railways were destroyed, and huge areas of land were made dangerous with landmines. In 1994, millions of people were killed in Rwanda as the Hutus fought the Tutsis, and hundreds of thousands of refugees fled across the borders to Zaire and Tanzania. In such circumstances, people think only of survival. They are not concerned with the environment, or wildlife. War is extremely damaging to the environment.

SAVING THE ELEPHANT

In 1979, there were about 1.3 million African elephants. Now there are fewer than half this number. During the 1980s, thousands were killed, mainly by poachers for the ivory tusks. In 1990, most countries agreed to ban any trade in ivory and this reduced the slaughter. Some countries now have a growing elephant population. In Kenya, the elephant herd is increasing by about 1,000 a year. The problem now is that elephants stray outside the reserves and cause great damage in the search for food.

Canada and Alaska

Animal at risk
One of the most beautiful birds of southern Canada is the whooping crane. It spent summer in the marshlands and lakes in the borderlands between Canada and the USA, then flew south in winter to the Gulf of Mexico. However, hunting and land drainage across North America virtually wiped it out. In 1944, there were just 15 or so left. A breeding programme seems to have saved them from extinction. Whooping cranes lay two eggs, but raise only one chick. By taking the spare egg and putting it into the nest of a sandhill crane, the second chick can be raised by foster parents. This tactic, and careful protection, has allowed the population of whooping cranes in Canada and the USA to rise to over 250.

Canada is the second-largest country in the world after Russia, but has only 29 million people. Most live in the south, in the cities and towns near the border with the USA. The southern region has rich farmland, and vast quantities of wheat are grown in the prairie states of Manitoba, Saskatchewan and Alberta. The summers are warm but short, and the winters are cold and long. Further north, where the climate is colder, there are huge conifer forests, called taiga. Further north still it is too cold for trees, and the soil beneath the ground remains frozen all year as permafrost. This damp, treeless landscape, or tundra, stretches across the hundreds of remote islands that reach up to the far north. The northern tip of Ellesmere Island is just 750km from the North Pole. The islands' only inhabitants are Inuit, who survive by hunting and fishing and, now, by importing food.

Alaska, bought by the USA from Russia in 1867, is the largest state of the USA. It shares the same cold climate as Canada, and much of the landscape is mountainous – including the highest mountain in North America, Mount McKinley (6194m).

These northern lands contain a vast range of wildlife, including huge herds of caribou, and many thousands of birds which come to the tundra in summer to breed. The ecology is still fragile and can be harmed by human activity, such as mining and forestry. Once there were vast shoals of fish off eastern Canada: now these have been almost wiped out by overfishing. Some people believe the seals are also responsible for killing too many fish and so, each year, thousands of baby seals are culled, or killed. But many ecologists argue that the seal cull is both cruel and unnecessary.

THE *EXXON VALDEZ*

Alaska has one of the world's most valuable oil fields, situated around Prudhoe Bay. A huge pipeline takes the oil right across Alaska to terminals at ports such as Valdez, where it is loaded onto tankers and shipped abroad. In March 1989, a supertanker, the *Exxon Valdez*, ran aground in Prince William Sound, spilling 50 million tonnes of crude oil into the sea. An oil slick 800km long spread out over the sea, and destroyed virtually all the wildlife in its path, including 36,000 sea birds and thousands of sea otters.

RECYCLING

The average family in the industrialized world produces a tonne of rubbish every year. Most cities in Canada run effective recycling schemes, separating and sorting waste and taking it to recycling plants.

USA

Grand Canyon,
Yellowstone National Park

Wetlands in Florida

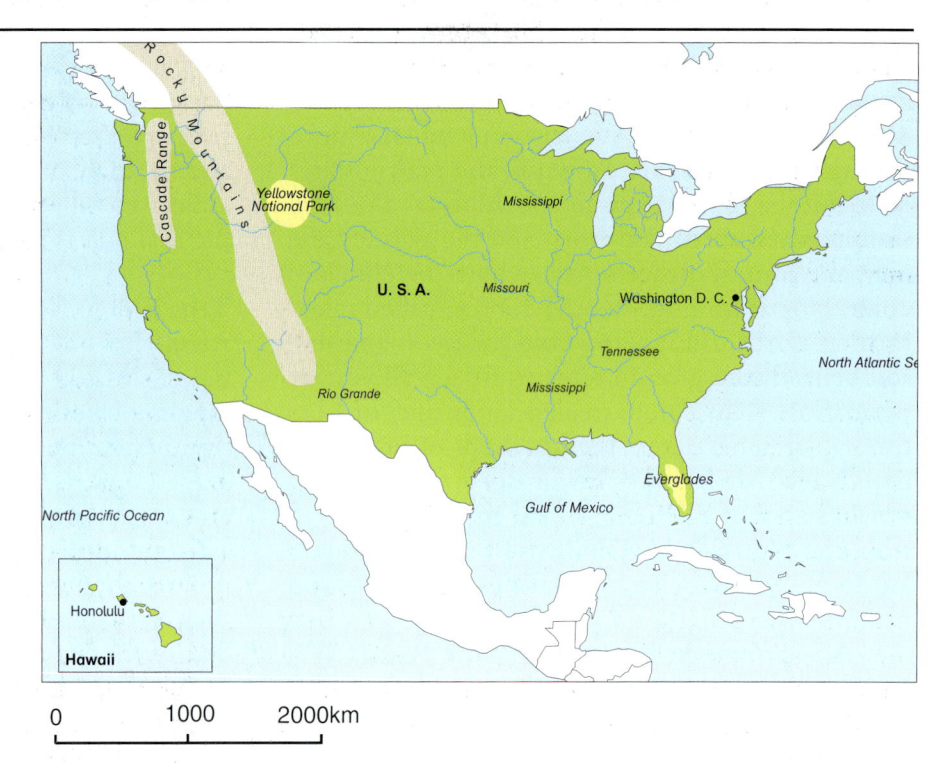

Animal at risk

The Caribbean manatee is a large aquatic mammal, a kind of sea cow which lives in the shallow seas and river estuaries along the coasts of Florida, the Caribbean islands and northern South America. Manatees are distant relatives of the elephant; adults can grow to about 4m and weigh half a tonne. They live in family groups, grazing on water plants. Unfortunately, their slow and gentle manner made them easy prey for hunters. Today manatees face greater threats from pollution and from motor boats, which cut them with their propellers. There are believed to be fewer than 2,000 left in Florida.

The United States of America is a land of great wealth, the headquarters of many of the world's biggest industries and companies, and a leader in technology.

The USA is still quite a new country. Most of the centre and west has been farmed and developed for little more than 100 years. Where once Native American cultures ruled, new settlers from the East Coast took over and so huge changes took place to the west of the Mississippi. Land which was open prairie, with huge herds of bison, has been converted into cattle ranches and wheat farms. Rivers have been dammed to provide water and power; new cities have sprung up. Forests have been cut down and replanted to provide timber, and mines have been dug to exploit the rich mineral resources.

America has magnificent mountains, forests and lakes in the Rocky Mountains, volcanoes in the Cascade Range, deserts filled with wind-sculpted rocks in the south-west, and mysterious swamplands in the south-east. But Americans consume huge quantities of energy to keep buildings warm in winter and cool in summer, and almost everyone drives to the huge shopping malls. This lifestyle produces a great deal of waste and has a direct impact on the environment. Many people in America are concerned to find the right balance between a comfortable and healthy lifestyle, and a healthy environment.

WETLANDS

Large areas of the south-east of the USA are covered by marshes and swamps, like the Everglades. Over the years, the wetlands have been drained to create farmland or to build on, and over half have now been destroyed. Wetlands contain a rich variety of wildlife which cannot survive elsewhere, and are among the richest ecosystems on earth. Draining wetlands threatens these animals with loss of habitat. In Florida, patches of dried-out land occasionally collapse into deep holes. Near the coast, salt water may seep in from the sea, making the land useless for farming. Upsetting the flow of water through the land can also cause flooding, while the loss of water can affect the amount of moisture in the air, and the climate.

NATIONAL PARKS

In 1872, Yellowstone, in north-west Wyoming, became the first National Park in the world. This magnificent area of mountains, forests, lakes, and volcanic springs and geysers, and its wildlife, was protected as a wilderness for the benefit of the people. The USA now has over 4,000 parks, and countries all over the world have followed suit.

MEXICO, CENTRAL AMERICA AND THE CARIBBEAN

Shops in Costa Rica

A street in Mexico

Animal at risk
Turtles are mysterious creatures, spending most of their lives at sea, and returning to land only to lay their eggs. They have long been threatened by humans, who have killed them for meat and collected the eggs as food. These days turtles are frequently trapped in fishing nets, where they drown. Kemp's ridley turtle was once commonly found along all the coast of North America from Mexico to the Canadian border. Today it is extremely rare, and a small, carefully protected strip of coastline in northern Mexico is now the only place where the female comes to lay her eggs.

With its white sand beaches lined with palm trees, coral reefs and blue seas, trees and bushes laden with colourful flowers, and volcanic mountains covered with tropical forest, this region is one of the most beautiful and spectacular in the world. The weather is generally hot, with plenty of rain, which is good for farming and plantation crops such as sugar cane, bananas and pineapples. The northern part of Mexico, on the other hand, is generally drier and, where there is little rainfall, there is desert.

Central America was once the homeland of a series of great civilizations, including the Olmecs, Maya and Aztecs. These came to an end with the arrival of the Spanish conquistadors in the early 16th century, and many of the Indian populations died in war and from diseases such as smallpox, brought by the Spanish. The Spanish ruled Central America and Mexico, and a number of the Caribbean islands. France, England and the Netherlands divided up the rest of the Caribbean islands, and thousands of slaves from Africa were imported to work on the sugar plantations.

Today most of the Caribbean islands are independent nations. History has left its mark in the variety of people and languages. The large populations, however, have made it hard for these countries to prosper and there is much poverty. So there is always pressure to develop the land, to chop down trees for timber, and to use old and polluting machinery and industrial techniques.

THE LURE OF THE CITY

Mexico City, the capital of Mexico, was built on the site of the old Aztec capital, Tenochtitlán, itself built on islands in the middle of Lake Texcoco. It is now one of the largest cities in the world, with a population of about 20 million, and may reach more than 24 million by the year 2000. The centre is surrounded by crowded, rubbish-strewn **shanty towns**, often without running water or sewerage. The air is so heavily polluted from industries and traffic, schools sometimes have to close because the air quality is so poor. Mexico City is also in a volcanic region, and in 1985 an earthquake killed 7,000 people.

TOURISM

Tourism can bring plenty of much-needed money to a poor country, but it can be a mixed blessing. Often, much of the profits go to tour operators and hotel owners, but tourism can bring benefits if it is carefully organized. In Costa Rica, the government has been able to use tourism to protect its wildlife. Visitors pay to visit the nature reserves, and now one fifth of the country is protected by these reserves.

NORTHERN SOUTH AMERICA AND BRAZIL

Tree felling in the jungle

Animal at risk
The jaguar lives in the forest and swamplands of the Amazon basin. A large, stealthy cat, similar in looks to the leopard, it hunts deer, wild pigs, monkeys, rats and other animals. Living largely on their own, except at mating time, jaguars need at least 5km² to hunt in. The destruction of the rainforest not only reduces their cover to hide in, but also their prey. Jaguars are also shot for their skins.

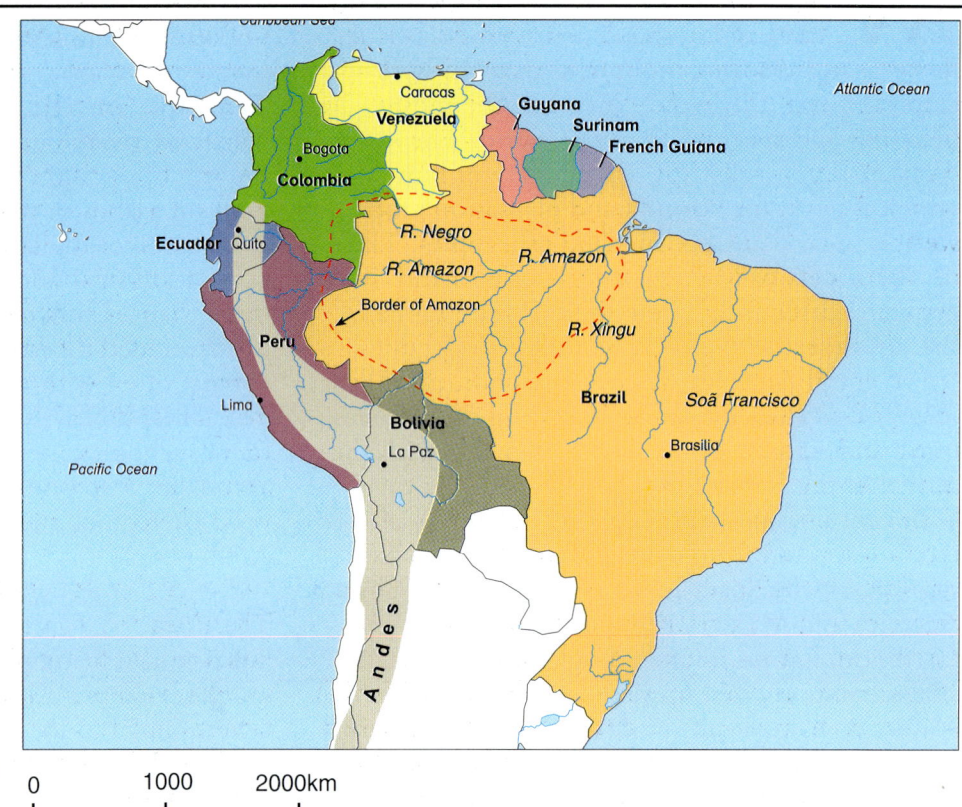

36

Northern South America has one of the richest and most varied landscapes of any region of the world. The northern coast lines the Caribbean Sea. In southern Venezuela the land rises up to great flat-topped mountains of the Guiana Highlands, where the Angel Falls tumble down 979m to form the highest waterfall in the world. The Andes stretch all the way down the western side of the continent, high enough for the peaks to remain snow-capped throughout the year, even on the Equator.

The most extraordinary feature of the region, however, must be the Amazon Basin, a huge plain crossed by dozens of sluggish rivers which flow into the Amazon, making it by far the biggest river in the world. It is so wide near its mouth that the shores cannot be seen from the middle of the river; and it is so deep that ocean-going ships can sail across South America to reach Peru. With its heavy rains and plentiful sunshine, the Amazon Basin contains more plants and animals than any other region in the world. But it also contains rich resources in timber, minerals and farmland, which are valuable to a poor nation such as Brazil. Many ecologists would like to see the Amazon Basin preserved as it is; the Brazilians hope it can make them rich. It has become one of the world's most active battlegrounds between **environmentalists** and developers.

Rainforest destruction

The Amazon Basin contains the largest rainforest in the world – equal to a third of all rainforest. It is said, however, that an area of forest the size of Scotland is destroyed every year in the Amazon Basin. One tenth has already gone. The trees are cut down for the timber; the cleared land can be used for agriculture or mining; or it may be flooded to create hydro-electric power stations. However, soon after the trees have been cleared away, the soil becomes too poor to grow crops. Burning creates massive air pollution and destroys the habitat of countless animals; forest peoples become homeless; and numerous rare plants are destroyed, some of which may be of great value to medicine. Already many medicines we use come from plants found in the Amazon forests.

rainforest reserves

The Brazilian government is aware of world concerns about the Amazon rainforest. Unfortunately, people pay for timber, minerals and farm products from the Basin, but no-one will pay the Brazilians for not destroying the forest. Under world pressure, however, the Brazilians have created a series of protected rainforest reserves

SOUTHERN SOUTH AMERICA

Cooking food on the street

Animal at risk

Chinchillas are rabbit-like rodents which live in the Andes. Their long, soft, blue-grey fur protects them from the cold – but also attracted hunters who killed them in their thousands to supply the fur trade abroad. In the early 1900s, various South American governments came together to save the chinchilla. Hunting was banned, and a programme of captive breeding was started. The result is that chinchillas have been saved, and today they number over 100,000.

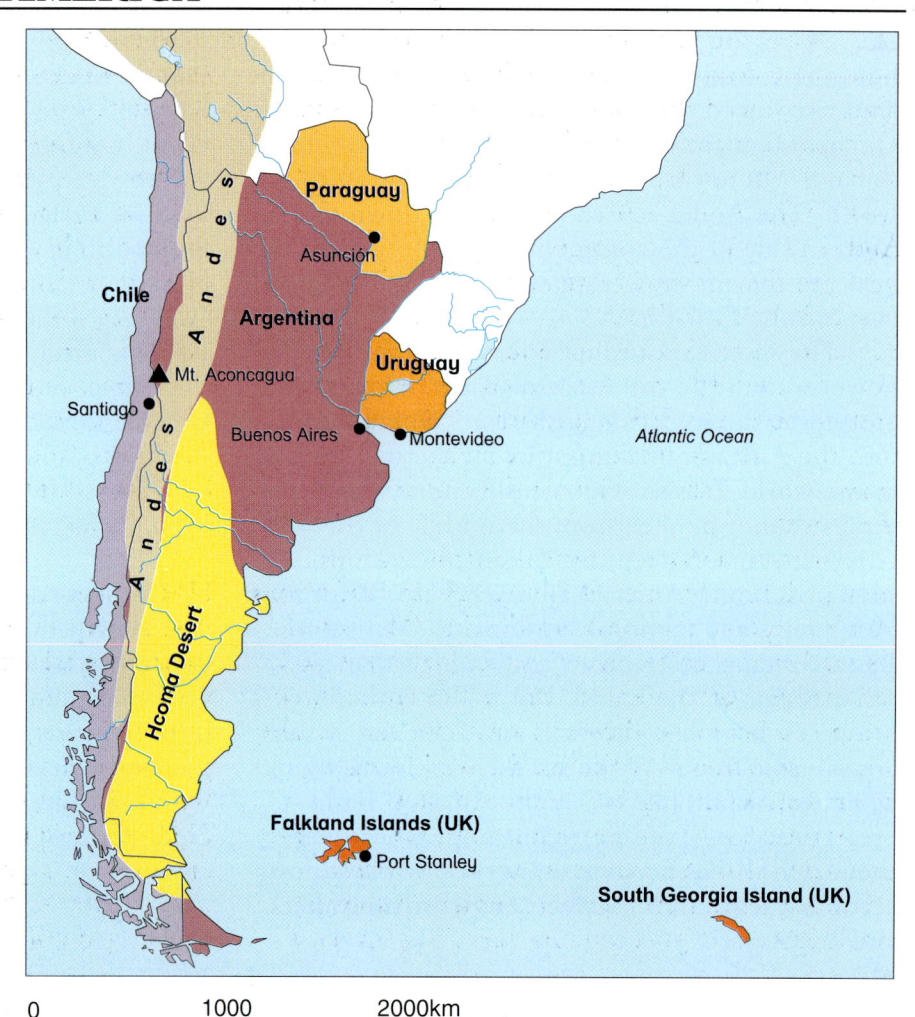

38

Stretching between the tropics and the Antarctic, Chile encompasses the great range of climate in this part of the world. The Atacama Desert in northern Chile is one of the driest regions of the world: in some parts no rain has been reported for the last 400 years. Throughout the length of the country, the land rises up from the coast to the high ridges of the Andes, including Mount Aconcagua, whose peak, just over the border in Argentina, is the highest in South America (6,960m). In the valleys around Santiago there are orchards and rich farmland. Further south the climate becomes more severe, with remote, uninhabited islands clustered against the coast, sheep-farming settlements and fishing ports. Punta Arenas is the southernmost town in the world.

Argentina shares almost the same mix of climate, but to the east of the Andes the land opens up into high plateaux and vast plains. The south is covered by the cold and dry landscape of Patagonia, but further north there are the rich grasslands, or pampas, where large herds of cattle are raised. The pampas stretches over the border into Uruguay, where cattle farming is a major industry.

These countries are rich in minerals and have excellent farmland, but each has suffered from political troubles during this century. However, new democratic governments seem to promise a period of greater stability and prosperity.

THE PROBLEMS OF DEBT

Many countries in the world suffer from debt. If a country buys more than it sells, then it will have to pay out more than it receives. To do this it borrows money, usually from other countries or the world's banks. But money is not lent free: interest is charged on the loan, and is payable every year. So the country which borrows money has to pay back not only the loan, but also the interest. Many countries have borrowed so much that they cannot pay it back – and can barely afford the interest. The result is that these countries are permanently in debt: it makes it very hard for them to invest in schools or hospitals or roads – or any environmental projects.

HYDROELECTRIC POWER

A relatively clean method of producing energy is **hydroelectric power**. By damming a river, the power of falling water can be harnessed to turn the turbines. Paraguay and Brazil co-operated to produce the massive Itaipú dam – and one of the world's largest stations – on the River Paraná. Hydroelectric projects do, however, have a major environmental impact. The lake behind the Itaipú dam destroyed the homes of 200,000 people and submerged one of the world's largest waterfalls.

Australia

An open-cast mine

© Chris Fairclough Colour Library

The Great Barrier Reef

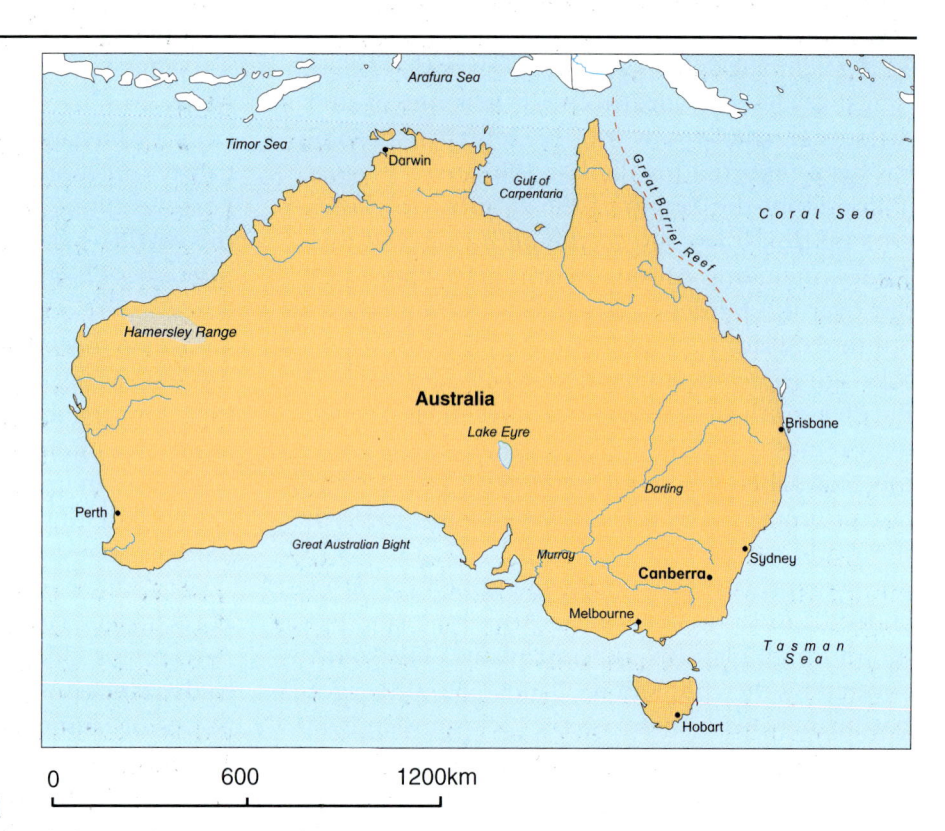

© John Noble Wilderness Library

Animal at risk

The numbat is a small marsupial which spends its life on the forest floor and in eucalyptus trees. It uses the claws of its front paws to burrow into termite nests, and its long, sticky tongue to lick up the insects. A numbat can eat 20,000 termites in a day. The destruction of its habitat to create farmland is the main reason why the numbat is now found only in a corner of Western Australia; also they have been killed off by **introduced species**, such as foxes and cats.

European settlers first came to Australia in 1788. Settlements spread along the south and eastern coasts, and isolated ports grew up in Western Australia and on the north coast. So little was known about the interior of the country that even fifty years after the first settlers arrived, some believed that it might contain a huge inland sea, like the Mediterranean. The Aborigines, however, knew the interior well: they had lived here for some 50,000 years.

Most of the middle of Australia is desert, crossed here and there by dry riverbeds which can flood after heavy rains. Sometimes the rainwater reaches hollows in the desert, which become temporary lakes, such as Lake Eyre, until dried by the sun again.

Australia's 17 million population lives mainly around the outer rim of the country. The desert is largely untouched, but around the rim lie a host of fragile environments affected by the growing human population. Some of the worst damage is done by bushfires, often started by carelessness; tree-felling threatens the tropical forests of northern Queensland; open-cast mines scour the dry landscapes of the north-west; and imported animals have also had some disastrous effects. Rabbits, introduced in 1858, threatened to overrun the grasslands until they were controlled in the 1960s. Today, the large, toxic cane toad, introduced in Queensland in the 1930s, has spread to the Northern Territory and New South Wales.

Mining

Australia mines many minerals, including iron, coal, bauxite, copper, lead, zinc, nickel and uranium. Because many of the mines are in remote areas, the mining industry has often shown little care for the environment. The Hamersley Ranges in the north of Western Australia contain the world's richest deposits of iron ore. Today the open-cast mines have reduced parts of the landscape to a maze of pits and vehicle tracks. The aluminium works near Port Pirie in South Australia are surrounded by a barren landscape smothered in red bauxite dust.

The Great Barrier Reef

The Great Barrier Reef stretches for 2,500km down the coast of Queensland in a chain of underwater reefs and coral islands – the largest construction made by living creatures in the world. For thousands of years, billions of tiny polyps have built up the banks of coral which are also home to 1,500 species of fish, 4,000 species of molluscs and 400 different kinds of corals. The Great Barrier Reef is now protected as a Marine Park.

NEW ZEALAND AND THE PACIFIC ISLANDS

Sheep droving

Animal at risk

The takahe is a large flightless rail, about the same size as a chicken. During the 19th century, hunters had **introduced species** of animals and killed them off quickly and by the 1890s, the takahe was thought to be extinct. Then, one day in 1948, an ornithologist discovered some surviving birds in the Murchison Mountains of the South Island. They have now been carefully protected, and some birds have also been released on islands where there are no predators. Their numbers have slowly increased to about 200.

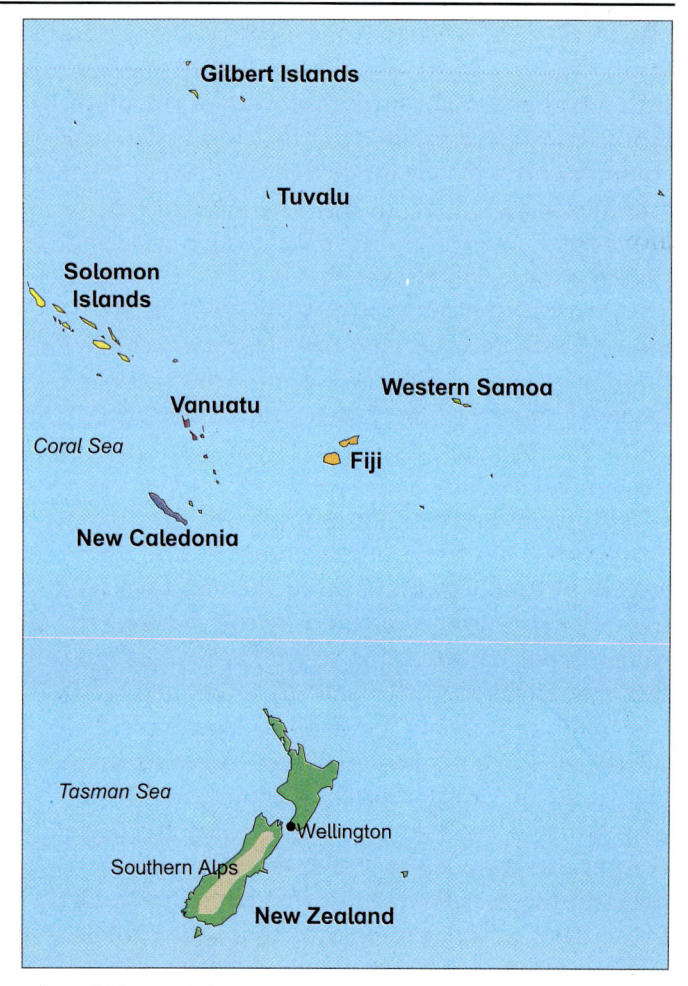

New Zealand is thought by many to be the most beautiful country in the world. The North Island – where most of the people live – has a coastline of bays and islands surrounding hilly land of forests and farmland, mountains and volcanic peaks. Much of the larger South Island is taken up by the Southern Alps, which rise to 3,765m at Mount Cook, the highest mountain of New Zealand.

With a population of just 3.5 million, the human impact on the environment of New Zealand may seem comparatively light. However, the impact of the animals introduced by humans has been considerable. Much of the landscape, for instance, has been made into sheep pasture: it is estimated that there are 17 sheep to every New Zealander. Most New Zealanders are highly committed environmentalists, and were fiercely opposed to the series of underground nuclear tests carried out by the French on the Polynesian island of Mururoa in 1995.

The Maoris, who settled in New Zealand over a thousand years ago, came from the Cook Islands, part of Polynesia. There are three main groups of islands in the South Pacific: Melanesia, Micronesia and Polynesia, each group settled by different sets of peoples. Today they live mainly by fishing, farming and tourism, and there is some light industry and mining. One of the great threats to South Pacific islands is global warming: if the sea level rises, many will lose a large part of their territory.

Animals from abroad

Before the Maoris came to New Zealand, bats were the only mammal, and birds could live safely on the ground, so many species lost the ability to fly. This included the kiwi, the national symbol, and the now-extinct moa, once the world's tallest bird, standing 3.5m tall. A form of rat brought by the Maoris attacked smaller flightless birds, reducing their numbers greatly. European settlers arriving in the 19th century brought cats, dogs, pigs and stoats, all of which made a number of other flightless birds extinct. Wherever humans bring new animals and plants they run the risk that the introduced species will change the ecology, sometimes disastrously.

Geothermal power

The North Island of New Zealand has one of the most famous sets of hot springs in the world, located around the city of Rotorua. Boiling hot water, heated by volcanic activity under the ground, bubbles to the surface in a series of hot lakes and geysers. Today many of the buildings in the city are heated in winter by steam from the hot springs and electricity is produced at specially designed power stations. **Geothermal energy** is considered one of the cleanest forms of energy.

ARCTIC (AND GREENLAND) AND ANTARCTICA

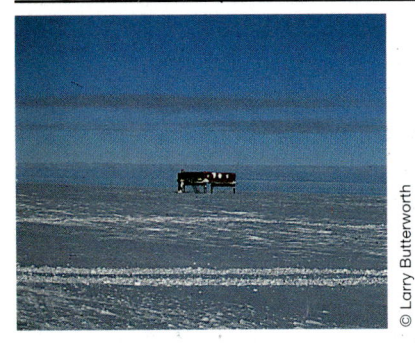

View of a research station

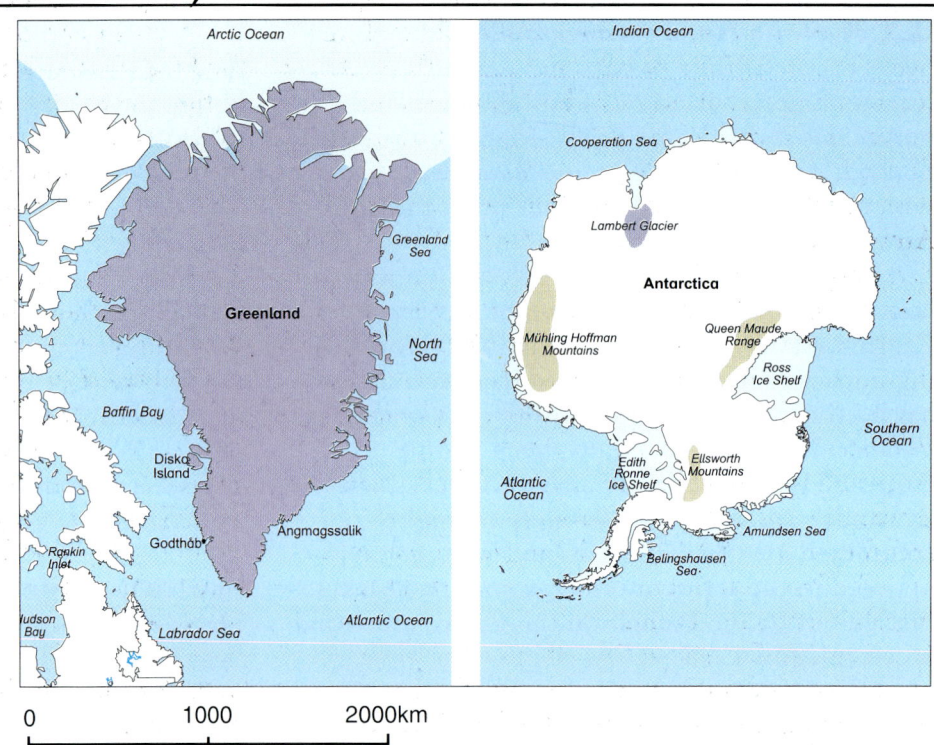

Animal at risk
During the 1960s it seemed that polar bears were in danger of extinction — mainly from hunters killing them for their fur. Their fur is very thick, and an effective form of insulation against the cold. These great bears roam around the Arctic ice floes in summer, in search of seals and other prey, which they can kill with a mighty swipe of the paw. In winter the females retreat to dens in the snow to give birth to their cubs. Hunting is now controlled and only limited numbers can be killed each year. There are about 40,000 left in the wild.

The Arctic is an ocean surrounded by land. In the middle of the ocean is an icecap, which floats on the sea and drifts with the ocean currents. The North Pole passes through the sea and the icecap: in 1958 the US nuclear-powered submarine, *Nautilus*, actually travelled through the North Pole under the ice. Each winter, when temperatures plummet and the Arctic Circle is plunged into months of complete darkness, the icecap expands and joins up with the land of northern Canada, Russia and Scandinavia.

The Antarctic, by contrast, is a continent; a high and mountainous piece of land covered with a layer of ice that is over 2km thick in places. Because land takes longer to warm up, the Antarctic is colder than the Arctic. The lowest recorded temperature in the world has been recorded here: -89°C. In winter the ice expands by 1,000km around the coasts of the Antarctic, hugely increasing its surface area.

Few life forms can live close to the poles, except for tiny mites and algae. But the coasts surrounding the icecaps are full of sea life, and attract large numbers of birds and mammals. The only humans living permanently in the polar regions are the Inuit and Eskimo peoples of the far north. Antarctica is uninhabited except for the teams of scientists who work at the various international research stations.

Although there is very little human activity in these regions, industrial pollution travels north and south on air and ocean currents and has entered the food chain. Traces of pollution have been found in polar bears' blood and penguin eggs, and the rich polar seas are threatened by increased fishing. International concern has been heightened and there is a now a strong desire to protect these regions.

THE OZONE LAYER

Ozone is a naturally occurring gas which forms a layer in the atmosphere at a height of 20km or more. Ozone gas in the atmosphere is vital as it blocks out harmful **carcinogenic** ultraviolet rays from the sun. Gases created by industry – particularly chlorofluorocarbons (CFCs) – damage the ozone. Recently holes, or thin patches, in the **ozone layer** have been found over the poles which appear to be getting larger, although many countries have now restricted the use of CFCs.

THE ANTARCTIC TREATY

In 1959, a group of 12 countries signed the Antarctic Treaty, agreeing not to mine for minerals or dump waste. The treaty stated that Antarctica should be used only for shared scientific research. In 1994, the Antarctic Treaty was renewed, this time signed by 42 nations, protecting the Antarctic once more.

GLOSSARY

acid rain rain (or snow) bearing very mild acids produced by air pollution (especially sulphur dioxide and nitrogen oxide)

alternative energy produced from renewable sources which does not involve burning fossil fuels or using nuclear fuels, and does not cause pollution

biodiversity the full range of plants and animals in any habitat

biodegradable will rot away and return to the earth through natural processes

captive breeding the breeding of animals in the protection of a zoo, usually to preserve an endangered species

carcinogenic causing the disease cancer

CITES Convention on International Trade in Endangered Species. An international agreement to prevent trade in living endangered animals and plants, or the products (such as fur) made from them

ecology the entire web of living things in any habitat, and their interaction with each other and their environment

effluent liquid waste products

endangered species any species whose numbers have become so reduced that there is a danger that it will become extinct

environment the surroundings of any living animal or plant

famine critical food shortage, which could lead to starvation

fertilizer product used to enrich the soil, to make plants grow better

fossil fuels fuels, such as, coal, oil and natural gas, that come from the ancient remains of plants and animals

fossil water water that has been trapped under the ground for millions of years

genetic engineering manipulation of the genes of plants and animals to produce new or altered species

geothermal power energy produced by using the heat of volcanic activity beneath the ground

global warming the gradual rise in world temperatures which has been observed over the last century

green the colour that has been adopted as a label to describe any product or activity which protects the environment

greenhouse effect the global warming that may be caused by a layer of carbon dioxide and other greenhouse gases in the atmosphere, which trap in the sun's heat

greenhouse gases the group of a dozen or so gases which are thought to be responsible for the greenhouse effect. Carbon dioxide is the most important; others include methane, oxides of nitrogen and chlorofluorocarbons (CFCs)

Green Revolution the rapid increase in agricultural produce which took place in many poorer countries after the 1960s

habitat the kind of environment in which an animal or plant lives

hybrid seeds seeds which have been specially developed by crossing specific strains of a plant

hydroelectric power electric power generated by the energy of falling water

introduced species any species of plant or animal that is brought into a country from abroad by humans

nuclear power power (usually electricity) produced by the immense energy released by splitting the atom, a process called nuclear fission

organic farming a method of farming that avoids the use of chemical fertilizers and pesticides

overfishing catching too many fish, with the result that the number of fish left to catch becomes smaller and smaller

ozone a naturally-occurring, poisonous gas which forms a layer in the atmosphere and protects the earth from the sun's harmful ultraviolet rays

pesticide any product which kills pests

radioactive fallout the dangerous radioactive pollution that occurs after a nuclear explosion

recycle to use again, especially things that would otherwise be thrown away

shanty town a poor area, usually on the outskirts of a city, where people have put up houses using whatever materials they can find

smog a harmful, fog-like mixture of air and air-borne pollution, found over some cities

solar energy energy produced by harnessing the power of the sun's rays

sustainable yield the amounts that can be taken safely from a natural resource (such as a forest) without harming its ability to recover, so that it can be used for ever

toxic waste poisonous waste products, such as dangerous chemicals thrown out after an industrial process

wetland an area of land covered by water and waterlogged soil, such as a marsh, bog or swamp

INDEX

Aborigines 41
Acid rain 3,13
Adriatic Sea 15
Afghanistan 19
Africa 27,29,35
    Central 28-29
    East 28-29
    North 26-27
    South 28-29
    West 26-27
Alaska 31
Alberta 31
Amazon basin 36,37
America 33
    Central 34-35
    North 27,31
    Northern South 31,36-37
    South 37,38-39,
Andes 37,39
Angel Falls 37
Angola 29
Antarctic 39,45
    Treaty 45
Antarctica 44-45
Arabian oryx - see Oryx
Aral Sea 19
Arctic 15,44-45
    Circle 45
Argentina 39
Arizona 18
Asia 17,21,25
    Central 17,18-19
    South 20-21
    South-East 24-25
Astrakhan 17
Atacama Desert 39

Australia 40-41
    Western 41
Aztecs 35
Baikal, Lake 17
Baikal nerpa - see Seal
Baikalsk 17
Balkans, the 14-15
Baltic Sea 15
Bangladesh 21
Bhopal 21
Biodegradable 4,5,6
Biodiversity 7
Black Sea 14,15,19
Bosnia 15
Bovine spongiform encephalopathy 11
Brahmaputra, river - see Jamuna
Brazil 36-37,39
British Isles, the 10-11
BSE - see bovine spongiform encephalopathy
Bulgaria 15
Canada 30-31,45
Captive breeding 7,38
Caribbean, the 32,34-35
    Sea 37
Cascade Range 33
Caspian Sea 19
Caucasus 19
Cellulose 17
CFC - see Chlorofluorocarbons
Chang Jiang, river 23
Chemical 6,13,17,21
Chernobyl 15
Chile 39
China 2,21-22,23
Chlorofluorocarbons 45
CITES 7

Climate 3,8,33,39
Coal 6,15,25,41
Convention on International Trade in Endangered Species 7
Cook Islands 43
Coral reef 25,35,41
Costa Rica 35
Coto Doñana 12
Croatia 15
Czech Republic, the 15
Desert 3,6,19,23,27,29
    semi 18,26,33,39,41
Desmoulin's whorl 10
Dodo 5
Drought 3,26,27
Ecology 13,23,31,43
Effluent 17
Electricity 4,15,23,27,43
Elephant 29,32
    African 29
Ellesmere Island 31
Empty Quarter - see Rub' al Khali
Endangered species 6,7,10,26
Energy 6,11,15,27,33
    geothermal 43
    sea tide 6
    solar 6
    wind 6
Environment 3,5,6,13,17,29,43
Equator 27,37
Eritrea 27
Eskimo 45
Ethiopia 27
EU - see European Union
Euphrates, river 19
Europe 12-13,15,16,25,27,43

European Union 13
Everglades 33
Exxon Valdez, the 33
Eyre, Lake 41
Factory 11,13,15,17,21,23,25
Famine 21,27
Farming 13,19,21,22,28,33,35,39,43
    Organic 13
Fertilizer 13,21,25
Finland 15
Fish 3,5,11,13,14,17,19,23,25,29,30,31,34,39,41,43,45
Flood 3,21,23,33,37,41
Florida 32,33
Forest 3,5,6,8,13,16,17,21,22,25,27,28,29,31,33,35,36,37,40,41,43
Fossil fuel 6,18
Friends of the Earth 6
Ganges, river 21
Genetic engineering 4
Geothermal energy - see Energy
Giant panda - see Panda
Global warming 8,43
Gobi Desert 23
Grain 4,10
Grassland 3,19,29,39,41
Great Barrier Reef, the 41
Great Britain 11
Green 3
    revolution 21,25
Green Great Wall 23
Greenhouse 4
    effect 8
    gases 6,8

Greenland 44-45
Greenpeace 6
Guiana Highlands 37
Gulf of Mexico - see Mexico
Gulf War - see War
Habitat 6,7,16,17,20,29,33,37,40
Hamersley Ranges 41
Himalayas 21
Horn of Africa 26,27
Houses
    back-to-back 11
    low-energy 15
Hungary 15
Hybrid seeds 21
Hydroelectric dam 23
Hydroelectric power station 39
India 20,21,24
Indian Ocean 21
Indonesia 25
Industrial Revolution 11
International Whaling Commission 9
Introduced species 40,42,43
Inuit 31,45
Irrigation 19
Itaipú dam 39
Jaguar 36
Jakarta 25
Jamuna, river 21
Japan 9,22-23,25
Java 24
Karakoram 21
Kazakhstan 17,19
Kenya 26,29
Kiwi 43
Korea 22-23
    North 23

47

South 23
Kuwait 19
Lead-free petrol - see
  Unleaded petrol
Madagascar 29
Magnitogorsk 17
Malaysia 25
Manatee 32
Manitoba 31
Maoris 43
Marine Park 41
Mauritius 7
Mediterranean 15,19,27
  Sea 14
Melanesia 43
Mexico 34-35
  Gulf of 30
Mexico City 35
Micronesia 43
Middle East 18-19
Monk seal - see Seal
Minerals 6,35,37,38,
  41,45
Mine 4,33,41,45
Mississippi 33
Moa 43
Mount Aconcagua 39
Mount Cook 43
Mount McKinley 31
Mount St Helens 3
Mozambique 29
Mururoa 43
Murchison Mountains 42
National Parks 33
Nature reserve 6,12,35
Nautilus, US 45
Newbury 10
New South Wales 41
New Zealand 42-43
Nigeria 27
North Island 43
North Pole 31,45

Northern Territory 41
Norway 9,15
Novosibirsk 17
Nuclear power 15
Numbat 40
Oasis 19,27
ocean 3,45
  current 8,45
Ogoniland 27
Oil 4,5,6,9,15,19,25,
  27,32
Olmecs 35
Oman 18
Oryx 18
Overfishing 5,6,14,25,31
Ozone
  gas 45
  layer 3,45
Pacific Islands, the 42-43
Pacific Ocean 17
Pakistan 21
Panda 22
Papua New Guinea 24-25
Paraguay 39
Paraná, river 39
Passenger pigeon 7
Patagonia 39
Perm 17
Permafrost 31
Pesticide 7,13,21
Philippines 25
Phoenix zoo 18
Poland 15
Polar bears 44,45
Polar ice cap 8
Pollution 3,4,5,6,7,8,11,
  13,14,15,17,19,21,
  25,32,37,45
Polynesia 43
population 4,6,9,10,11,
  13,20,22,25,26,29,

30,34,35,41,43
Port Pirie 41
Prince William Sound 31
Project Tiger 20
Prudhoe Bay 31
Punjab 21
Punta Arenas 39
Queensland 41
Radioactive
  fallout 15
  waste 15
Rain 3,13,19,21,27,
  35,37
Rainforest 6,8,21,25,29,
  36,37
Recycling 5,6,31
Refugee 28,29
Research station 45
Rhinocerus 24
  Great Indian 24
  Javan 24
  Sumatran 24
Rocky Mountains 33
Romania 15
Rotorua 43
Rub' al Khali 19
Russia 15,16-17,17,
  31,45
Rwanda 28
Sahal countries 26-27
Sahara Desert 27
Santiago 39
Saskatchewan 31
Saudi Arabia 19
Scandinavia 14-15,45
Scientist 4,8,15,45
Seal 31,44
  Baikal nerpa 17
  Monk 14
Senegal 27
Shanty towns 35

Sheep 16,27,39,43
Siberia 16,17,23
Sichuan 22
Singapore 25
Slovenia 15
Snow 3,37,44
Soil erosion 27
Solar energy 6,27
Somalia 27
South Island 42,43
Soviet Union 15,17
Spain 12
Spanish imperial eagle 10
Sudan 27
Sustainable yield 5,25
Sweden 15
Takahe 42
Tanzania 29
Tenochtitlán 35
Texcoco, lake 35
Thailand 25
Thames, river 11
Tigris, river 19
Tourism 35,43
Toxic cane toad 41
Toxic waste 7,25,27
Traffic 11,13,37
Turkey 19
Turkmenistan 19
Turtles 34
  Kemp's ridley 34
Uganda 28
Ujung Kulon 24
Ukraine 15,17
Union Carbide 21
United Nations
  troops 27
Unleaded petrol 6
Ural Mountain 17
Uruguay 39
USA 3,7,18,25,30,

31-32, 33
Uzbekistan 19
Valdez 31
Venezuela 37
Vietnam 24
Virunga Mountains 28
Wales 15
War 5,29,35
  Civil 28,29
  Gulf 19
  Second World 15,
  23,29
Water, fossil 19
Wetland 29,31
Whale 9
  blue 9
  humpback 9
  sperm 9
Wolf 16
World Wide Fund for
  Nature 6
Wyoming 33
Yangtze
  Gorge 23
  Valley 23
Yangtze Kiang, river -
  see Chang Jiang
Yellowstone 33
Yemen 19
Yugoslavia 15
Yunnan 22
Zebra 29
  plains 29
  mountain 29
  Grevy's 29
Zaire 28,29